OPPOSING VIEWPOINTS® SERIES

Pacifism

Other Books of Related Interest:

Opposing Viewpoints Series

Extremism

At Issue Series

What Is Humanity's Greatest Challenge?

Current Controversies Series

Torture

“Congress shall make no law . . . abridging the freedom of speech, or of the press.”

First Amendment to the U.S. Constitution

The basic foundation of our democracy is the First Amendment guarantee of freedom of expression. The Opposing Viewpoints Series is dedicated to the concept of this basic freedom and the idea that it is more important to practice it than to enshrine it.

OPPOSING VIEWPOINTS® SERIES

Pacifism

Noah Berlatsky, Book Editor

GREENHAVEN PRESS
A part of Gale, Cengage Learning

GALE
CENGAGE Learning™

Detroit • New York • San Francisco • New Haven, Conn • Waterville, Maine • London

GALE
CENGAGE Learning™

Christine Nasso, *Publisher*
Elizabeth Des Chenes, *Managing Editor*

For more information, contact:
Greenhaven Press
27500 Drake Rd.
Farmington Hills, MI 48331-3535
Or you can visit our Internet site at gale.cengage.com

Articles in Greenhaven Press anthologies are often edited for length to meet page requirements. In addition, original titles of these works are changed to clearly present the main thesis and to explicitly indicate the author's opinion. Every effort is made to ensure that Greenhaven Press accurately reflects the original intent of the authors. Every effort has been made to trace the owners of copyrighted material.

Cover Image copyright iStockPhoto.com/Wilshire Images.

LIBRARY OF CONGRESS CATALOGING-IN-PUBLICATION DATA

Pacifism / Noah Berlatsky, book editor.
p. cm. -- (Opposing viewpoints)
Includes bibliographical references and index.
ISBN 978-0-7377-5229-8 (hardcover) -- ISBN 978-0-7377-5230-4 (pbk.)
1. Pacifism. I. Berlatsky, Noah.
JZ5548.P33 2011
303.6'6--dc22

2010038262

Printed in the United States of America
1 2 3 4 5 6 7 15 14 13 12 11

Contents

Why Consider Opposing Viewpoints?

> *"The only way in which a human being can make some approach to knowing the whole of a subject is by hearing what can be said about it by persons of every variety of opinion and studying all modes in which it can be looked at by every character of mind. No wise man ever acquired his wisdom in any mode but this."*
>
> *John Stuart Mill*

In our media-intensive culture it is not difficult to find differing opinions. Thousands of newspapers and magazines and dozens of radio and television talk shows resound with differing points of view. The difficulty lies in deciding which opinion to agree with and which "experts" seem the most credible. The more inundated we become with differing opinions and claims, the more essential it is to hone critical reading and thinking skills to evaluate these ideas. Opposing Viewpoints books address this problem directly by presenting stimulating debates that can be used to enhance and teach these skills. The varied opinions contained in each book examine many different aspects of a single issue. While examining these conveniently edited opposing views, readers can develop critical thinking skills such as the ability to compare and contrast authors' credibility, facts, argumentation styles, use of persuasive techniques, and other stylistic tools. In short, the Opposing Viewpoints Series is an ideal way to attain the higher-level thinking and reading skills so essential in a culture of diverse and contradictory opinions.

In addition to providing a tool for critical thinking, Opposing Viewpoints books challenge readers to question their own strongly held opinions and assumptions. Most people form their opinions on the basis of upbringing, peer pressure, and personal, cultural, or professional bias. By reading carefully balanced opposing views, readers must directly confront new ideas as well as the opinions of those with whom they disagree. This is not to simplistically argue that everyone who reads opposing views will—or should—change his or her opinion. Instead, the series enhances readers' understanding of their own views by encouraging confrontation with opposing ideas. Careful examination of others' views can lead to the readers' understanding of the logical inconsistencies in their own opinions, perspective on why they hold an opinion, and the consideration of the possibility that their opinion requires further evaluation.

Evaluating Other Opinions

To ensure that this type of examination occurs, Opposing Viewpoints books present all types of opinions. Prominent spokespeople on different sides of each issue as well as well-known professionals from many disciplines challenge the reader. An additional goal of the series is to provide a forum for other, less known, or even unpopular viewpoints. The opinion of an ordinary person who has had to make the decision to cut off life support from a terminally ill relative, for example, may be just as valuable and provide just as much insight as a medical ethicist's professional opinion. The editors have two additional purposes in including these less known views. One, the editors encourage readers to respect others' opinions—even when not enhanced by professional credibility. It is only by reading or listening to and objectively evaluating others' ideas that one can determine whether they are worthy of consideration. Two, the inclusion of such viewpoints encourages the important critical thinking skill of objectively evaluating an author's credentials and bias. This evaluation will illuminate an author's reasons for taking a particular stance on an issue and will aid in readers' evaluation of the author's ideas.

It is our hope that these books will give readers a deeper understanding of the issues debated and an appreciation of the complexity of even seemingly simple issues when good and honest people disagree. This awareness is particularly important in a democratic society such as ours in which people enter into public debate to determine the common good. Those with whom one disagrees should not be regarded as enemies but rather as people whose views deserve careful examination and may shed light on one's own.

Thomas Jefferson once said that "difference of opinion leads to inquiry, and inquiry to truth." Jefferson, a broadly educated man, argued that "if a nation expects to be ignorant and free . . . it expects what never was and never will be." As individuals and as a nation, it is imperative that we consider the opinions of others and examine them with skill and discernment. The Opposing Viewpoints Series is intended to help readers achieve this goal.

David L. Bender and Bruno Leone,
Founders

Introduction

> *"[Reinhold] Niebuhr's great foe was idealism. American idealism, he believed, comes in two forms: the idealism of noninterventionists, who are embarrassed by power, and the idealism of imperialists, who disguise power as virtue."*
>
> *—David Brooks,*
> Atlantic, *September 2002*

Protestant theologian Reinhold Niebuhr was a major modern thinker on issues of war and peace. In particular, his 1940 essay "Why the Christian Church Is Not Pacifist" was one of the most important arguments in favor of Christian support for US involvement in World War II. The essay has been widely influential to both Christians and non-Christians.

Niebuhr's argument is that the Christian Church is not and should not be pacifist. Rather, "Christianity is a religion which measures the total dimension of human existence not only in terms of the final norm of human conduct, which is expressed in the law of love, but also in terms of sin." For Niebuhr, then, Christ calls human beings to love and peace but recognizes that in a flawed world both love and justice are required. Christian pacifists, Niebuhr argues, are utopians, who believe that human beings are essentially good. They therefore mistakenly believe that love and peace can be brought into being purely through human effort. Niebuhr argues, on the contrary, that humans are innately sinful and that "justice can be achieved only by a certain degree of coercion on the one hand, and by resistance to coercion and tyranny on the other hand." In short, Christian pacifists have too much faith, not in Christ, but in human beings. Niebuhr maintains that Christianity has a deeper understanding of human nature and knows that force and coercion must sometimes be used to guard against anarchy and tyranny and to promote justice.

Despite this stance, Niebuhr does not completely reject pacifism. Rather, he argues that pacifists can testify to, and be a reminder of, the importance of love. He notes,

> We who allow ourselves to become engaged in war need this testimony of the absolutist against us, lest we accept the warfare of the world as normative, lest we become callous to the horror of war, and lest we forget the ambiguity of our own actions and motives and the risk we run of achieving no permanent good from this momentary anarchy in which we are involved.

Niebuhr's realist view of war has been taken up by many thinkers, both religious and nonreligious. In fact, both supporters and opponents of the Iraq war used Niebuhr to justify their positions. Paul Elie, writing in the November 2007 issue of the *Atlantic*, noted that

> the Niebuhr revival has been perplexing, even bizarre, as people with profoundly divergent views of the war have all claimed Niebuhr as their precursor: bellicose neoconservatives, chastened "liberal hawks," and the stalwarts of the antiwar Left. Elie adds that understanding Niebuhr remains important because he "got to the roots of the conflict between American ideals and their unintended consequences, like those the United States now faces in Iraq."

One of the thinkers who has been influenced by Niebuhr is President Barack Obama. In an interview with David Brooks in the April 26, 2007, *New York Times*, Obama said that he had learned from Niebuhr

> the compelling idea that there's serious evil in the world, and hardship and pain. And we should be humble and modest in our belief we can eliminate those things. But we shouldn't use that as an excuse for cynicism and inaction. I

> take away . . . the sense we have to make these efforts knowing they are hard, and not swinging from naïve idealism to bitter realism.

Those themes were evident in Obama's Nobel Peace Prize acceptance speech delivered on December 10, 2009, in which he said,

> I know there is nothing weak—nothing passive—nothing naïve—in the creed and lives of [Mahatma] Gandhi and [Martin Luther] King. But as a head of state sworn to protect and defend my nation, I cannot be guided by their examples alone. I face the world as it is, and cannot stand idle in the face of threats to the American people. For make no mistake: evil does exist in the world.

Thus Obama, like Niebuhr, noted the power and worth of nonviolence while simultaneously insisting that evil sometimes requires nations to resort to force.

While Niebuhr's view of war and peace has gained many converts, it has also been criticized, especially by pacifists. One of the leading theologians to take issue with Niebuhr's ideas was John Howard Yoder, a Mennonite and, therefore, a member of one of the historic peace churches. In his 1994 book *The Politics of Jesus*, Yoder argues that those such as Niebuhr are in error when they claim that Christianity is intended to provide a means to practical politics. Instead, Yoder says that

> what is usually called "Christian pacifism" is most adequately understood not on the level of means alone, as if the pacifist were making the claim that he can achieve what war promises to achieve, but do it just as well or even better without violence. This is one kind of pacifism, which in some contexts may be clearly able to prove its point, but not necessarily always. That Christian pacifism which has a theological basis in the character of God and the work of Jesus Christ is one in which the calculating link between our obedience

> and ultimate efficacy has been broken, since the triumph of God comes through resurrection and not through effective sovereignty or assured survival.

Thus, for Yoder, the duty of a Christian is not to balance love and judgment to obtain the best realist outcome, as Niebuhr and Obama suggest, but rather to follow the example of Christ, lead where it may.

Opposing Viewpoints: Pacifism further explores the conflict between pacifism and realism, both in a religious and a secular context, in chapters titled What Is the Relationship Between Christianity and Pacifism? How Do Other Religions View Pacifism? What Are Secular Pacifist Traditions? and What Is the Link Between Pacifism and Political and Social Issues? The arguments advanced by thinkers such as Niebuhr, Yoder, and Obama continue to influence thinking on pacifism and war today.

OPPOSING VIEWPOINTS® SERIES

CHAPTER 1

What Is the Relationship Between Christianity and Pacifism?

Chapter Preface

Among the Christian denominations with the strongest commitment to pacifism are the historic peace churches (HPC). The term specifically refers to the Church of the Brethren, the Religious Society of Friends (or the Quakers), and the Mennonite churches. The three churches "all have held an official witness that peace is an essential aspect of the gospel and all have rejected the use of force and violence," according to Sara Speicher and Donald F. Durnbaugh in the 2002 revised edition of the *Dictionary of the Ecumenical Movement.*

The Mennonites are the oldest of the HPC. They were originally a radical Protestant group who grew out of Anabaptism in Holland in the mid-sixteenth century. The Amish, a well-known religious denomination that rejects modern technology and dress, broke away from the Mennonites in the late 1600s. The Mennonites in general do not separate themselves from modern society as the Amish do. Instead, "the Mennonite church emphasizes service to others as an important way of expressing one's faith. A disproportionately large number of Mennonites spend part of their lives working as missionaries or volunteers helping those in need, nationally or internationally," according to an article by John D. Roth on the website of the Mountain Community Mennonite Church. Pacifism is central to Mennonite faith.

The Religious Society of Friends, or the Quakers, was a radical Puritan movement founded in seventeenth-century England by George Fox, who believed that Christians could have a direct personal experience of divine revelation. As a result, the Quakers' tradition emphasizes individual revelation and spiritual seeking and has few doctrinal requirements for all members. Nonetheless, the Quakers have a strong tradition of social justice. "The origins of Christian abolitionism [opposition to slavery] can be traced to the late 17th century and the Quakers," according to a BBC article updated July 3, 2009. In addition, "simplicity, pacifism, and inner revelation are long-standing Quaker beliefs," according to B.A. Robinson in a December 26, 2009, essay on the website Religious Tolerance.

The Church of the Brethren has its roots in Germany at the beginning of the eighteenth century. Brethren beliefs included adult baptism and a strong focus on the word of the New Testament. Though the Brethren have historically been committed to peace, the commitment to nonviolence can take different forms. Ronald J. Gordon noted in a March 1996 essay, now available on Church of the Brethren Network website, that

> although the official position of the Church of the Brethren through the discernment of Annual Conference historically resists war and all forms of violence, there is intellectually honest disagreement throughout the denomination concerning the interpretation of peace and nonresistance. There are some Brethren who resist any involvement with the military while others enlist and serve without reservation. Some Brethren deduct the military spending percentage from their federal income taxes while others pay in full. You will find Brethren opinions scattered all along the political spectrum from doves to hawks.

Before the twentieth century in the United States, members of the historic peace churches (including other Anabaptist groups as well as Mennonites) were the only individuals who could qualify for conscientious objector status—that is, they could be exempted from military service on religious grounds. The law changed during World War II, but even at that time "conscientious objectors were still predominately members of the historic peace churches," according to Karl Nelson in the winter 1999 issue of *Pietisten*.

During the war in Vietnam, conscientious objection became seen as a matter of individual conscience, and membership in an HPC became less important. In addition, other churches with strong pacifist commitments, such as Jehovah's Witnesses and Seventh-Day Adventists, have grown in influence. However, the historic peace churches continue to bear a central Christian witness to peace. The following viewpoints explore that witness as well as objections to it from the perspectives of both members of the peace churches and others.

VIEWPOINT 1

"Utopian pacifism may appeal to seminary campuses, book fairs, and religious online chat rooms. But mainstream Jewish and Christian ethics have always chiefly addressed the real world, not an imagined ideal."

Christian Pacifism Is Unrealistic and Immoral

Mark D. Tooley

Mark D. Tooley is president of the Institute on Religion and Democracy and author of Taking Back the United Methodist Church. *In the following viewpoint, Tooley argues that the pacifism of the religious Left is little more than an unwarranted surrender to Islamic terrorism. He argues that Christian ethics have always recognized the necessity for some state-sanctioned violence to ward off chaos. He concludes that utopian pacifism is built on contempt for America and hostility toward Israel.*

As you read, consider the following questions:

1. What led Aaron Taylor to change from a conservative evangelical to a pacifist, according to Tooley?

Mark D. Tooley, "Evangelical Pacifism in the War on Terror," *FrontPage Magazine*, December 31, 2009.

2. According to the viewpoint, of whom is Taylor a disciple?
3. What does Taylor's jihadist interlocutor say he dislikes about Christianity and democracy?

The new evangelical Left largely agrees with the old religious Left that traditional religious conservatives have distorted the Bible with their patriotism, support for America's wars, and friendship for Israel. For left-leaning evangelical elites, no less than for old mainline Protestant bureaucrats, pacifism, at least for America, is the answer.

Surrender Is Not Christian

A new voice for evangelical pacifism is a young missionary named Aaron Taylor, who writes for Jim Wallis's *Sojourners*, and who recently authored the book *Alone with a Jihadist*, which argues that Christian pacifism is the right retort to radical Islam. Is surrender to Islamic terror the only correct Christian response? For Taylor, as for increasing numbers of evangelical elites who reject traditional Christian just war[1] teachings, the answer tragically is "yes."

"The version of Christ we have in America, especially white evangelicalism, is so huge with nationalism and patriotism, so fused together, we need a radical separation," Taylor surmised in a recent interview. Too many religious conservatives take biblical "verses out of context to justify . . . American wars," he fretted. "When it comes to invading sovereign nations, or Israel bombing Gaza and hundreds of civilians dying," we need to "switch the burden of proof around," he urged.

Apparently Taylor was previously a traditional conservative evangelical. But his 2006 participation in a film documentary by leftist Canadian director Stephen Marshall about Christian-

1. Just war teachings are traditional Christian guides to when and how war may morally be fought.

ity and Islam post-9/11 [September 11, 2001, terrorist attacks on America], called *Holy Wars*, brought him together with an Irish convert to radical Islam. In the jihadist [a radical Muslim committed to holy war], Taylor wearisomely "saw a mirror image of my own side, militant evangelical Christianity," "support for Israel and America," and the "same militancy I see a lot of on Christian television." His encounter with the radical Muslim that supposedly so reminded him of conservative American evangelicals was a "traumatic experience" that motivated his appeal for Christian pacifism in *Alone with a Jihadist*.

In a recent column for *Sojourners*, Taylor naturally lashes out at President [Barack] Obama's troop surge in Afghanistan [in 2009], which he found disturbingly reminiscent of George W. Bush, if somewhat "less arrogant." Still, Taylor opined that Obama's "rejection of unilateralism, his willingness to dialogue with enemies, and his understanding of the limits of power—howbeit nuanced—make him about as good of a president as we can expect on the foreign policy front given the current state of American culture and, more specifically, the American Church."

America's Supposed Love of War

Americanism militarism, Taylor has discovered, originated with America's "civil religion of God, guns, and country," which seduces even liberals into "glorifying military heroes and showing off the Pentagon's latest weapons technology." America's supposed love of war will not change until "the words 'fighting for freedom' become more associated in the average American mind with strikes, boycotts, and voter registrations than with ground invasions and bombing raids."

Like many left-leaning evangelicals, Taylor is a disciple of the late Notre Dame teacher and Mennonite [a Christian denomination often associated with pacifism] theologian John Howard Yoder, who claimed that the demand for nonviolence

Pacifism and Anti-Americanism

The religious Left's . . . pacifism is typically only concerned about restraining U.S. military efforts and does not usually quibble with aggression or oppression by tyrants, even when genocidal.

Equating justice with reflexive anti-Americanism is old hat for the religious Left . . . who, . . . preside over a dwindling flock that no longer seriously heeds their political posturing.

Mark D. Tooley,
"Methodist Bishops Urge Surrender in Afghanistan,"
FrontPage Magazine, *November 25, 2009.*
http://frontpagemag.com.

was the central message of Christ's crucifixion. Yoder's devotees, most prominently Duke Divinity School teacher Stanley Hauerwas, insist that pacifism should be Christianity's defining tenet. They reject the just war tradition that has guided the vast majority of Christians, based on Church Fathers like St. Augustine, and St. Paul's admonition in Romans 13 that God has ordained the state to "wield the sword" against evil.

"What if John Howard Yoder replaced Augustine as the intellectual giant of the Western Church?" Taylor dreamily asked in his *Sojourners* piece. "For that to happen, a lot more Bible-believing Christians are going to have to be convinced that Romans 13 is not a carte blanche for Christians participating in state-sanctioned violence, that the Old Testament is a poor pretext for just war theory, and that John the Baptist wasn't condoning violence when he didn't tell the Roman soldiers of their day to give up their occupations."

Like most Christian pacifists, Taylor boasted that his approach is "radical." And he is untroubled by his break from most Christian tradition, complaining that Protestant Reformers [of the 16th century] Martin Luther and John Calvin "didn't go far enough," but the "people who did were the Anabaptists [Christian denomination associated with pacifism]," or the spiritual ancestors of Mennonites, Quakers, and Amish. Apparently Taylor's seven-hour meeting with a militant jihadist was enough to persuade him that most of Christianity was wrong about government's vocation to protect its people from violence and terror. Historically, most Mennonites and Quakers have allowed others to fight their wars without condemning them. But the new breed of evangelical Left Anabaptist wannabes insist they must denounce people of faith who appreciate police and militaries as moral necessities in a fallen and turbulent world.

Taylor's jihadist interlocutor complained to him that Christianity and democracy failed to create "godly government" and allow evil to "run rampant," by not executing homosexuals and adulterers, among other omissions. Of course, thousands of years of Jewish and Christian tradition have addressed how faith should interact with governance. But Taylor seems largely to ignore these moral teachings, or portray them in caricatures, with his website asserting that "many Christians support warmongering and unnecessary bloodshed rather than peacemaking." His website describes his discovery of pacifism grandly as the "solution to end all religious/quasi-political warfare." Purportedly, "many fundamentalist/evangelicals tend to ascribe [sic] to a Zionist[2] theology, which believes that it is good to be at war with anyone who opposes the Christian Right, to expedite the glorious return of the Messiah, there is one crusader, Aaron Taylor, who believes otherwise."

Surrendering to Chaos

The evangelical Left, so ashamed of the patriotism of traditional religious conservatives, believes that its own brand of

2. Zionism is the Jewish movement to establish and support the state of Israel.

absolutist pacifism will cleanse the American church of its warmongering sins and ultimately, perhaps, redeem America from its supposed thirst for bloodshed. Taylor's website claims that if "Christians everywhere were to return to their pre-Augustine heritage of nonviolence as a way of life, then the social impact of the church would be greater than that of the Protestant Reformation."

Such utopian pacifism may appeal to seminary campuses, book fairs, and religious online chat rooms. But mainstream Jewish and Christian ethics have always chiefly addressed the real world, not an imagined ideal. Historic Christianity empowers the state to repress, where possible, crime and terror, not surrender to chaos. But for many on the evangelical Left, contempt for America, and for Israel, override fidelity to historic Christian beliefs.

> *"Ultimate loyalty belongs to Christ for the Christian, not to the state. Therefore if the state asks a kind of allegiance that the Christian cannot give, the Christian will refuse to obey the state."*

Christian Pacifism Confronts Hard Moral and Practical Questions

Mennonite Church Canada

Mennonite Church Canada is a Canadian church with thirty-seven thousand members. It is part of the Mennonite denomination, which is known for its commitment to nonviolence. In the following viewpoint, the author argues that pacifism provides practical, though not always perfect, answers to difficult questions. The church notes that nonviolence has been an effective strategy to resist oppression and injustice in many instances. The viewpoint also insists that pacifism cannot guarantee a particular outcome in any conflict, just as war does not guarantee success. Pacifism is chosen because it is the teaching of God, maintains the church, which Christians should follow as best they can. The first twelve points in this article were originally created for the Mennonite Church Canada website Alternative Service in the Second World War (www.alternativeservice.ca/hard/).

As you read, consider the following questions:

1. What does the viewpoint say is the flip side to the statement "the Nazis would have won the war if everyone else had been a pacifist"?
2. What does the viewpoint say that pacifist Christians would like to do with taxes that currently go to fund the military?
3. According to the prophet Jeremiah, how are strong nations measured?

Below are some common, valid, and difficult questions nonviolent peace builders have faced. The answers are not simple or short. Military force and intervention is too often a way of speeding towards a resolution—an attempt to solve conflict quickly. Great patience, and sometimes nonresistant sacrifice of life, is required to solve conflict by nonviolent means.

Cowardice Is Not the Issue

1. What is the difference between being a pacifist and a coward? There are pacifists who could be cowards and there may be soldiers who are cowards. But that is not the issue. It may actually take less courage to enlist in the military than to refuse to do so, especially when there is pressure or incentives to enlist. It takes even more courage to resist the draft when the government of the land is actively recruiting and drafting people who would not enlist out of their own accord. Some countries threaten imprisonment (or worse) for persons who resist the draft. It takes courage to resist such threats.

2. The Nazis would have won the war if everyone else had been a pacifist. The flip side to this statement is that if everyone were a pacifist, there would be no war. It is unrealistic to think that Christian pacifists exist only in one nation and not in another. If, at a minimum, Christians all over the world would take a position of refusing to use violence in solving problems, it would make a huge statement to political leaders and international relations. In the long run, there is a better chance that the spiral of violence could be broken by refusing to meet violence with violence. In the case of the Nazis, read the compelling story on one person who mobilized his community in France to nonviolently resist the Nazis. "André Trocmé argued that 'decent' people who fail to respond to the humiliation and destruction of others around them because of indifference or cowardice pose the most dangerous threats to the world."

3. *Why aren't all Christians pacifists? Why would Christians go to war if Jesus taught us to love our enemies?* Most Christians know that Jesus taught us to love our enemies. Some believe that nonviolence applies only to their personal lives, and that the state has the right to defend itself through violent means. Some Christians hold the pacifist position to be unrealistic. Other Christians believe that the state is the highest good and must of necessity be preserved. Anything that does not meet this requirement is judged to be unrealistic. And yet other Christians hold that a distinction needs to be made between just and unjust wars and that Christians should participate in fighting just wars. These continue to be areas of disagreement with Christian pacifists.

4. *Are all Mennonites [that is, members of the Mennonite denomination, a historically nonviolent church] pacifists?* No. Many young Mennonite men enlisted in the world wars. Some were not yet ready or prepared to take a stand at age eighteen. They had not come to a strong enough conviction on the matter to resist the draft. Others were enticed by the propaganda that promised them glory and honour and a vocation or trade at the end of their term of service. Many were lured

into service in the military. But others who did enlist have become even stronger in their peace values after their military experience.

How Can a Pacifist Fight for Justice?

5. If war isn't the answer, what can we do to fight injustice and oppression? We can start with our relationships among families and friends. We can act justly and seek justice for others. The more we refuse to oppress people ourselves and stand up for the oppressed people of the world, the less need there would be for war. It is especially important to address the way richer nations exploit poorer nations economically and socially. It is important also to unmask the real reasons for war. So often wars are fought not to remove injustice and oppression but to make it possible for such injustices to continue. It is a real service to the nation to be critical of all unjust policies and action of the nation.

6. What would a pacifist do if someone attacked his or her family? It is important that we create conditions that preempt violence in all relationships, and when things do escalate, to choose the nonviolent options open to us. However, pacifists are human like everyone else. Failure to do what is right does not make the wrong right.

Duty to the State

7. How can you live in Canada and then not fight to defend it? What does it mean to be a good Canadian citizen? Why do you not obey the government? By doing what is right I am defending Canada. By giving my life to justice and peace I am supporting what is basic to the welfare of the nation. War is not necessarily good for the country as is assumed in the question. What is right and just exalts a nation. To live by a higher standard is to be a good citizen. Ultimate loyalty belongs to Christ for the Christian, not to the state. Therefore if the state asks a kind of allegiance that the Christian cannot give, the Christian will refuse to obey the state.

8. Aren't your taxes going to support the military? Isn't that like praying for peace and paying for war? Peace-building Christians are not against the government of the nation. They are not against taxes as such. They believe in supporting the legitimate programs of the government. They do not want to support war and other programs that are counterproductive to the nation. They would very much like to contribute the amount contributed to the military to a special peace fund that would be used for international aid and other causes that would contribute towards peace and goodwill. The government on its part, however, does not want to specify which taxes support war and which do not because this would make it too easy for many people to object to war taxes. War taxes remain hidden as much as possible. We would like to have all governments honour their citizens by allowing those who are pacifists to contribute their taxes to a pool of taxes that are used for humanitarian causes within the country and beyond.

9. Is it ever right to go to war? When you take the position that war itself is wrong, it is not possible to justify any war.

Pacifism and Idealism

10. Pacifism and nonviolent resistance is too idealistic and it would never work on a large scale. This statement assumes that we have to achieve a certain end and pacifism does not guarantee a certain end. But that is not the point. War too does not guarantee a certain outcome. It only professes to do so. As Christians, it is our calling to do what is right and to stand up for what is right. Because of our faith, we can leave the outcome to God. Because of the biblical record and stories from our own past, we know that God can use our feeble efforts to achieve certain ends—but we may not know when. Our task is to attend to the means and not to guarantee ends. But there are examples in recent history of nonviolent resistance that has brought about change: witness the Orange Revolution in Ukraine (2004–05), the opposition to apartheid in South Af-

Mennonites and Nonviolent Resistance

Since World War II there has also been an increased interest in social justice in many Mennonite churches in Canada. People who emphasize this aspect see justice and peace as interconnected, and often use the Hebrew idea of "Shalom" (peace, well-being) to support their views. . . .

Proponents of social justice often believe that the church's prior commitment not to "resist evil" (nonresistance) led Mennonites to be inactive. Instead, many propose "nonviolent resistance," where the church challenges injustice, but refuses to use violence in doing so.

King of Glory Mennonite Church, "Mennonite History." http://mennonite0.tripod.com.

rica, the civil rights movement in America, and the Gandhi-led movement for India's independence from Great Britain. See the film *A Force More Powerful* for more examples.

11. How did pacifists think that Adolf Hitler, the dictator of Germany, would be stopped or defeated? Christians in East Germany resisted government directives in many and subtle ways. When the collapse of the Soviet regime came, the banner in the victory parade in East Germany read: "Wir danken dir Kirche!" or "We thank you, Church!" The silent but persistent resistance of the church was recognized and honoured by the population. If more people would have spoken with their lives and if the church had not been, to a degree, in complicity with Hitler, the program against the Jews might not have happened the way it did. Hitler could have been defeated in his program if the people had not played his game.

12. Why should I care about pacifists when soldiers sacrifice so much more? In fact, pacifists have sacrificed their lives—but there are many more soldiers who do so. And since military might is the predominant worldview, we hear more about the risks and sacrifices soldiers make via the mainstream media. Nonviolent peace builders are increasingly acknowledging that they need to take the same risks in working for peace as does a military that seeks peace through force. A recent story about pacifists who made a sacrifice comes from the war in Iraq. American Tom Fox of Christian Peacemaker Teams lost his life in Iraq, when he and fellow peace workers James Loney, Norman Kember, and Harmeet Singh Sooden were taken hostage. Though rescued by the military, this was not their choice; they knowingly committed their lives as a sacrifice for their beliefs. They knew what they were getting into, they knew this could happen, and they had previously agreed that in such a situation, they would not seek to be rescued by force. Many others in history have made the difficult choice to risk death for their beliefs, as recorded in the *Martyrs Mirror*. . . .

Old Testament Warfare

13. If you believe we are called to live for peace then how do you explain all the warfare in the Old Testament? This is a good question, and one that peace-building and peace-acting Christians are often called to defend.

Indeed, there is a lot of human warfare and forceful oppression cited in the Old Testament. But it does not necessarily follow that this is how God intends things to be.

The creation stories of Genesis 1 and 2 in the Old Testament set the foundation and God's ideal for peaceful living. Out of the chaos and darkness God calls creation into being with the power of words rather than violent force. Very quickly though, personal violence and warfare enter the human story; but this is the result of the fall of humanity, not the will of God. In the great exodus, God chooses to advocate for the

Hebrew people (Exodus 14:14), not with conventional military means but by plague and pestilence (Exodus 7–15). While these acts are still violent by our present-day standards, their miraculous nature hints at what will only be more fully revealed in Jesus Christ; namely that the way God saves and delivers us is not by reliance on human warfare. The difficult but appropriate role of the Hebrew people is to trust God's methods and not the methods of military leaders to deliver them.

The Hebrew people of the Old Testament respond to God's desire in a number of ways. At times they are obedient and allow God to save them using God's ways (God's victory at Jericho, Joshua 6). At times they cooperate and assist God (the battle of Ai, Joshua 8) and at times they resort to full military preparation and human fighting which is a failure of faith and trusting in God (the battles of King David).

While the Hebrew people experience war and inflict warfare on other nations, the Old Testament criticizes warfare: When the Hebrew people demand to have a human king to rule them as other nations have (1 Samula 8), God reminds them of the oppressive nature of kingship and military might.

As an expression of sacred desires for humanity, God chooses prophetic leaders who are outside conventional political and military structures. The prophet Isaiah speaks of a time when the nations will not fight and when the tools of war will be transformed into productive farm implements that provide for the needs of people (Isaiah 2:1–4). Prophets like Jeremiah proclaim that in God's view, strong nations are not measured by military might but for how they care for the most vulnerable in society—the refugee, the orphan, and the widow (Jeremiah 22:1–5).

God's ultimate redemptive strategy has nothing to do with the conventions of human force and warfare. God's method is that of the suffering servant found in Isaiah 40–55. From a human perspective this is suicide. But God's strategy is both mysterious and miraculous: God's servant will suffer rather than cause others to suffer and in that suffering God will be victorious and the world will come to experience the peace that God desires for all of us.

Viewpoint 3

"Where the Christian pacifist can simply dismiss any Christian participation in violence . . . the Christian who intends to follow the just war tradition has a moral obligation actually to apply the criteria."

Christian Pacifism Offers a Strong Challenge to the Just War Theory

William Witt

William Witt is an associate professor at Trinity School for Ministry. In the following viewpoint, he argues that pacifism, especially as elaborated by theologian Richard Hays, presents a strong challenge to just war theorizing. Pacifism is based on emulating Jesus, Witt says. Commonsense arguments against pacifism, such as those advanced by author C.S. Lewis, are therefore not convincing. He notes that other kinds of arguments may call pacifism into question but concludes that the just war tradition must account for the fact that many wars supported by Christians have not, in fact, been just.

As you read, consider the following questions:

1. How does Witt define natural law?
2. What does Witt say is the fundamental Christian pacifist claim about facts?
3. Witt says that Christian pacifist sects viewed themselves not as converting the greater society but as doing what?

Richard Hays [theologian and author of the 1996 book *The Moral Vision of the New Testament*] represents an approach to Christian ethics that follows in the tradition of Mennonite John Howard Yoder and Methodist ethicist Stanley Hauerwas. This ethical approach understands Christian ethics to have a specific content provided by the New Testament texts themselves. Christian ethics is not simply a reiteration of ethical principles known by everyone in general (natural law). Nor is Christian ethics simply a matter of drawing practical application from abstract theological principles like law and gospel. Finally, the narrative texts of the New Testament do not present an "impossible ideal" meant to show human shortcomings, an "ethic of perfection" for select Christians, or an "interim" ethic reflecting a "consistent eschatology" concerned only with the end of the world—all views amounting to the claim that New Testament ethics are not relevant to the lives of contemporary Christians.

The Christian Story and Just War Theory

One of the distinctive characteristics of this approach is its narrative emphasis. The narrative mode of the New Testament documents is understood to have moral content. The gospels tell a story and Christian ethics has to do with appropriating the Christian story for one's own. . . .

However, this narrative approach has been a challenge to at least one reading of Christian ethics, the just war theory.[1]

1. Just war theory is a Christian tradition that provides criteria for when and how to conduct wars.

The story of Jesus is a story of nonviolence and nonresistance. Jesus conquers the powers of evil not by raising up an armed rebellion, but by going to the cross. God the Father vindicates him by raising him from the dead; the paradigm for Christian discipleship is that of "imitating Christ," and the classic Christian ideal is that of the martyr. Hays's exegesis follows in the earlier steps of John Howard Yoder and Stanley Hauerwas who argued in their works *The Politics of Jesus* and *The Peaceable Kingdom* that following in Jesus' nonviolent way of the cross demands a nonviolent ethic.

Hays is clear about the problems that this narrative approach to Christian ethics creates for traditional "just war" ethics. He says that the "just war criteria" are not derived from, nor derivable from the New Testament. They depend on a process of "natural law" reasoning that has little biblical warrant. In Hays's words: "[T]he New Testament offers no basis for ever declaring Christian participation in war 'just.'" Accordingly, Hays concludes that the just war tradition . . . has to be rejected as incompatible with the teaching of the New Testament.

This is a fairly serious objection. If the just war tradition is incompatible with the central narrative structure of the New Testament, it would seem that Christians who wish to make the Jesus story their story must embrace pacifism.

A Challenge to the Pacifist Stance

Has Hays made his case for Christian pacifism and against the classic just war tradition? I am not convinced that he has. Yet I am not happy that advocates of the traditional just war position adequately address the issues he raises. . . .

First to be examined is an essay by [novelist and Christian apologist] C.S. Lewis, "Why I Am Not a Pacifist." Lewis was one of the most popular Christian apologists of the twentieth century who also wrote numerous essays on Christian ethics, including this one. His essay is helpful because it represents just the kind of "commonsense" argument that is often raised against Christian pacifism.

At first read, Lewis's argument does indeed seem to be a classic case of "natural law" reasoning [that is reasoning based on human understanding, rather than on truth revealed in scripture]. . . .

Confirmation that Lewis is arguing for a "natural law" critique of pacifism is his initial claim that the source of moral judgments is conscience. Fundamental to conscience seems to be a collection of what Lewis calls "intuitions," which are "inarguable," and are "such that no good man has ever dreamed of doubting." These intuitions include "ultimate preferences of the will for love rather than hatred and happiness rather than misery." Combined with these "intuitions" are "process[es] of argument" by which one arranges the intuitions to convince someone that a particular act is wrong or right. Lewis says such processes are "highly arguable." In addition, there are the facts themselves about which one raises moral questions or makes moral judgments. Finally, in order to exercise humility in judgment, there should be respect for previous authority as well, what we might prefer to call "tradition."

Lewis states the process by which one comes to a reliable moral judgment as follows: (1) The facts are clear and little disputed; (2) the basic intuition is unmistakable; (3) the reasoning that connects the intuition to a particular judgment is strong; (4) there is agreement (or at least not disagreement) with authority. If the above four criteria are met, then one can have "moral certainty" about an action.

Lewis then applies the four criteria to the question of pacifism and finds it wanting.

The Goals of Pacifism

On the question of fact, Lewis suggests that all agree that "war is very disagreeable." The contrary claim made by pacifists, he claims, is that "wars always do more harm than good." Lewis rejects this point as "merely speculative." There simply is no way to know whether wars always do more harm than good. (But Lewis does seem to go beyond this claim. He ventures that "history is full of useful wars as well as useless wars.")

Is this, in fact, the fundamental factual claim that Christian pacifists make? One at first is tempted to reject it as a caricature, but Hays does, in fact, seem to say something like this. He says a "serious case can be made, that, on balance, history teaches that violence simply begets violence." To the hoary test case of resistance to [German dictator Adolf] Hitler, Hays responds with his own question: "What if the Christians in Germany had refused to fight for Hitler? . . . The long history of Christian 'just wars' has wrought suffering past all telling, and there is no end in sight."

But, rhetoric aside, I do not believe that the fundamental Christian pacifist claim about facts is that "wars always do more harm than good." Rather, I think the fundamental pacifist claim is a rejection of the consequentialist ethics assumed in such a claim. That is, the rightness or wrongness of participating in war is not decided by the outcome of the decision in terms of its consequences in terms of tangible goods, but in terms of moral consequences. Some acts should not be done regardless of their possible benefits. One thinks, for example, of rape or torture or the deliberate taking of innocent human life. The historic ethical stance that I think even Lewis would have embraced would be that rape, torture, or the deliberate taking of innocent human life should be avoided regardless of their tangible consequences in terms of concrete goods because such actions are inherently morally repugnant. I think the pacifist argument is somewhat the same in regard to acts of violence. And, of course, the facts that a Christian pacifist like Hays appeals to are not the facts of the perceived consequences of certain violent or nonviolent actions, but the facts of a certain kind of community. The story initiated by the life, death, and resurrection of Jesus Christ is one of the nonviolent confrontation of and redemption of evil. Those who make this story their own must live as Jesus did. . . .

Finally . . . Lewis demonstrates a real misunderstanding of the motivations of those whom he criticizes when he imagines that the goal of pacifists is political—to recruit enough people to the pacifist vision so that finally war will become impossible. Lewis responds to this goal by noting that only liberal societies tolerate pacifists, and that the most likely result of a large number of recruits to pacifism in such communities would be the inability of the liberal community to defend itself against those societies that do not tolerate pacifists. The long-term result, then, of a large number of recruits to the pacifist cause would be a world in which there were no pacifists.

Whatever one might think of a certain kind of utopian secular pacifism, Christian pacifism has usually been embraced by Christian sects who viewed themselves not as converting the greater society as a whole to their pacifist vision, but as providing a nonviolent alternative to the violence of surrounding cultures, e.g., the Mennonites [a Christian denomination long associated with nonviolence]. Hays's Christian pacifism is just such an alternative. The vision of church he embraces is that of a "community of peace," an alternative to a church "deeply compromised" by nationalism, violence, and idolatry.

Pacifism and Authority

This brings us to the final point of Lewis's critique of pacifism, that having to do with authority. And, here, I think Lewis scores a few points. First, Lewis notes correctly that the pacifist is at odds with human authority in general: "To be a pacifist," he says, "I must part company with Homer and Virgil, with Plato and Aristotle, with Zarathustra and the *Bhagavad-Gita*, with Cicero and Montaigne, with Iceland and

Christians Can Hold Their Military Accountable

The American military is reportedly filled with Christians. What if those Christians actually paid attention to their tradition's prohibitions on unjust fighting in war? Imagine the witness to be had if the churches taught their flocks the virtue of fighting justly and demanded strict penance from those who did not. Imagine the witness the churches would give if their members refused to participate in certain bombing missions in, say, Iraq, if innocent people were directly targeted. Imagine the scene of even one Christian soldier standing trial for refusing to bomb citizens or shoot prisoners. Now *that* would be an effective witness. More than that, it would serve as a real litmus test for Christians trying to decide if their nation is the type of nation that fights just wars.

Darrell Cole, "The Problem of War," Touchstone, *April 2003. www.touchstonemag.com*

with Egypt." I would think that, for the Christian pacifist, parting ways with all of these pagan worthies would not be particularly disturbing. After all, the Christian community is supposed to be an alternative community to the ways of the world. Augustine most famously contrasted *The City of God* and *The City of Man*. However, Lewis points out correctly that the pacifist also parts company with Christian authority. He points to the Thirty-Nine Articles, to Protestants, to Catholics, to Thomas Aquinas, to Augustine. Lewis is mistaken, however, when he claims that "all bodies that claim to be Christian—those who claim apostolic succession and accept the Creeds—have constantly blessed what they regarded as righteous arms." While the majority of the Christian tradition has rejected pacifism, there have been exceptions, and highly honorable ones. One thinks, of course, of the historic peace churches like the Mennonites, but also, of celebrated individual Christians like St. Francis, Martin Luther King, Jr., Dorothy Day [a 20th-century American Catholic journalist and social activist]. (Hays rightly points to these people as praiseworthy examples.) Just as significant, a good case can be made that the pre-Constantinian [before A.D. 300] patristic church was pacifist. Origen [an early Christian scholar], for example, argued against the pagan Celsus [2nd-century Greek philosopher] that Christians do not take up arms. They pray for the emperor. They will not fight for him. The office of soldier was one of the offices that early Christians had to renounce when they were baptized. Moreover, the exemption of clergy from military service seems to hearken back to an understanding that bloodshed was incompatible with a perfect following of Christ. Nonetheless, Lewis has a point. The vast majority of Christian history and tradition has seen the soldier's role as an honorable one, and when Christians were no longer persecuted by the state, they did not hesitate to take public office, and a new role that did not exist before came into being, the Christian soldier.

This brings us to Lewis's last point, which, if he were making a Christian argument, should, I think, have been his first. That is, what do the biblical texts actually say? Lewis concedes that the "whole case for Christian pacifism" rests on "certain dominical utterances," specifically, the commands in the Sermon on the Mount [from the New Testament] not to resist evil and to turn the other cheek. Interestingly, Lewis rejects the possible interpretation that Jesus' command is hyperbole, a way of saying that we should "put up with a lot." Lewis thinks that the text means "exactly what it says," but with certain reservations that the hearer would understand without having to be told so. Specifically, Lewis understands the commands of nonresistance are absolute when understood to apply to injuries to myself and to any temptation I might have to retaliate. But the problem changes when other factors intervene. Lewis asks whether Jesus' hearers would have understood him to mean that one should simply stand aside and do nothing if a homicidal maniac attempted to murder a third party. Again, Lewis's argument supposes that the only alternative to allowing a homicidal maniac to murder his victim is to use violence, but his reading is, I think, a possible reading of the text. . . .

The Challenge to Just War

Hays makes a superb case for understanding the New Testament community as a community that must live a certain kind of life, modeled on the character of Jesus, who chose the cross over the sword. At the same time, however, the church is not the only community. Both Old and New Testaments recognize governments as having a limited role in executing justice, a role that the church cannot fulfill. . . .

However, this does not get the Christian advocate of just war off the hook when it comes to answering the question of whether a Christian can partake in war. Where the Christian pacifist can simply dismiss any Christian participation in violence as inconsistent with what it means to follow Jesus, the Christian who intends to follow the just war tradition has a moral obligation actually to apply the criteria. Hays is right that Christians have been particularly compromised by repeatedly participating in wars that do not come close to meeting just war criteria. In our contemporary setting, one needs to ask questions like: Can a preemptive war ever be consistent with just war criteria? Is it permissible to engage in war on the basis of a fear of what one's enemies "might do"? What are a nation's obligations when it goes to war based on presumptions about "weapons of mass destruction" that turn out not to exist after all?[2] Are weapons that indiscriminately kill

2. America invaded Iraq in 2003 based on the assumption that Iraq had nuclear, chemical, or biological weapons of mass destruction. Such weapons were not found after the invasion.

civilians and non-civilians alike like cluster bombs and land mines permissible to use in warfare? If it is permissible to invade a hostile nation for its ostensible possession of weapons of mass destruction, how can we justify our own possession of such weapons? If torture is inherently immoral, have Christians already failed when they argue about whether actions like waterboarding [an interrogation technique involving controlled drowning, widely seen as torture until it was used by the George W. Bush administration following the September 11, 2001, terrorist attacks on the United States] really constitute torture? Is it morally permissible to imprison people for years without trial and without charges because we have determined ahead of time that they must be terrorists when it is only the trials and charges that we have denied them that could determine whether they really are? The list is a long, and uncomfortable one.

"Both just war and pacifism put peace in the center of their ethical thinking, and relegate war to the margins."

Churches Should Move Beyond the Pacifism/Just War Argument

Paul Rasor

Paul Rasor is director of the Center for the Study of Religious Freedom at Virginia Wesleyan College. In the following viewpoint, he speaks to the Unitarian Universalist community, a church that has roots in the Christian faith and includes Christian members but whose membership is largely post-Christian. Rasor argues that just war theory and pacifism converge in a commitment to nonviolence and that both have a presumption against war at the center of their thinking. Rasor concludes that the liberal Unitarian Universalist church should embrace nonviolence in such a way that neither pacifists nor those who embrace just war thinking are excluded. This viewpoint was published prior to the Unitarian Universalist Association's formal adoption of the Statement of Conscience on Creating Peace,

Paul Rasor, "Beyond Just War and Pacifism: Toward a Unitarian Universalist Theology of Prophetic Nonviolence," *The Journal of Liberal Religion*, vol. 8, pp. 20–24, 2008.

which occurred at the 2010 General Assembly. The Statement can be found at www.uua.org/socialjustice/socialjustice/statements/13394.shtml.

As you read, consider the following questions:

1. Why does Rasor say he prefers to use the term "nonviolence" rather than "pacifism"?
2. According to Rasor, prophetic nonviolence takes a principled stand against what official presumption about young people?
3. What question about his proposal does Rasor say haunts him?

In this [viewpoint], I develop my proposal that we move beyond just war[1] and pacifism by adopting an integrated model I call *prophetic nonviolence.* To move "beyond just war and pacifism" is not to abandon either tradition; it is rather to recognize that both perform important roles in our ongoing efforts to reduce the violence of war. My starting assumption is that the pacifist and just war approaches complement and reinforce each other as strategies of denunciation and critique. As [philosopher and theologian] James Childress has observed:

> Just war theorists need pacifists to remind them of their common starting point: the moral presumption against force and war. And pacifists need just war theorists to provide a public framework for debates about particular wars and for the restraint of the practice of war.

A Commitment to Nonviolence

I begin, then, with a fundamental commitment to nonviolence. Unitarian Universalism [a liberal religious tradition with Christian roots] has never been a peace church [that is, a

1. Just war is a theological tradition that provides criteria for determining when and how Christians should engage in war.

church devoted to pacifism], but we have always affirmed peace as among our most basic values and for two centuries pacifists have found a home in our congregations. We have always been involved in work to create the kinds of just communities out of which peace emerges, and we have long supported the use of nonviolent methods of conflict resolution at all levels, including conflict among nations. This is the legacy we share with the traditions of nonviolence and pacifism. At the same time, Unitarian Universalism has always been an *engaged* religion, one that is involved in the world and that tries to make a difference in the world. An important dimension of this involvement is our tradition of speaking prophetically—of bringing reasoned judgment and critique to bear on the social conditions that generate injustice and violence. In the context of war and the use of military force, this part of our tradition has been well served by the restrictive just war model.

My proposal for *prophetic nonviolence* draws on both dimensions of our tradition by linking our deep commitment to nonviolence with our historical practice of prophetic social critique. It is also supported by the deeper commonalities between the pacifist and just war traditions. Before examining these commonalities in detail, however, I want to comment on my rejection of the traditional terms. I . . . [note] the problematic nature of the term "just war," and I agree with [minister and scholar] Walter Wink that this term is oxymoronic in its implications. Moreover, I want to emphasize the tradition's role as a strategy of denunciation and critique, and the term *prophetic* does this.

I prefer *nonviolence* in part because it is broader in scope than "pacifism." It suggests a consistent response to issues of violence in domestic and cultural contexts. . . . In addition, using *nonviolence* helps avoid the implication that we are aligning ourselves with the peace churches, which, as I noted earlier, seems inappropriate. Walter Wink prefers the term nonviolence because for him, "'pacifism' sounds too much like 'passivity.'" I do not share this association, perhaps because of my own experiences with Quaker pacifists, who are anything but passive. . . .

Links Between Just War and Pacifism

There are several important commonalities or "points of convergence" between just war and pacifism that support my integrated approach to *prophetic nonviolence.* [Professor] Richard Miller . . . argues that the presumption against war shared by both traditions "can be expressed as the duty of nonmaleficence," or the duty not to harm. This duty encompasses a sense of "compassion for those who are victims of harm, a bias against suffering, an intolerance of cruelty," convictions shared by both traditions. We [Unitarian Universalists] can recognize these duties as among our own deepest religious values, expressed in our affirmations of the inherent worth and dignity of all persons and of justice, equity, and compassion in human relations.

A second point of convergence is that both just war and pacifism put peace in the center of their ethical thinking, and relegate war to the margins. For the just war approach, this has been both a clear priority and a potential problem. Theodore Koontz [a professor of ethics and peace studies] argues that the just war model tends to lose sight of its own central peace norm by focusing its analytical energy on the marginal cases. Miller points to the same problem and argues that just war advocates, along with their pacifist cohorts, "should work more assiduously to make the requirements of peace central to moral discourse and practice." Keeping peace in the center helps focus our critique. It can also remind us of the importance of extending our prophetic practice to include peacemaking and other prevention strategies. In other words, a critique of war is incomplete if it stops with denunciation. In my model of *prophetic nonviolence*, practices of denunciation imply a duty to contribute to effective peace practices.

Making Nonviolence the Norm

Third, both just war and pacifism are concerned with the limits of loyalty to the state. This is more obvious in pacifism, especially religious forms of pacifism, which often explicitly frame their responses to the government's war efforts in terms of a higher loyalty to God. But Miller notes that this concern is present in the just war model as well. By placing the burden of proof on those who would justify the use of force, the presumption against war reflects a basic suspicion of official claims. The result is that the just war model is "structured to resist the kinds of claims that states may make in the name of necessity." Joseph Fahey [a professor of religious studies] makes the important point that "today's nation states presume that young men and women are willing to kill other young men and women for their flag." This presumption is reflected in our national policies toward conscientious objection, among other things. Killing is considered the norm, and an individual must make a case for not killing. By incorporating the counter-assumption in both the pacifist and just war traditions, *prophetic nonviolence* takes a principled stand against the official presumption that young people must be prepared to kill at the behest of the state.

Finally, I want to note a historical convergence suggested by the recent trend toward nonviolence in the non-peace churches. In a significant departure from tradition, Roman Catholic teaching now recognizes just war and nonviolence as "distinct but interdependent methods of evaluating warfare." Traditionally, Catholic pacifists were held to be outside official church teaching. In 1965, however, the Second Vatican Council [a meeting to determine and reformulate doctrine] expressly accepted pacifism as a legitimate stance for individual Catholics, reversing centuries of official doctrine. The American bishops extended this in 1993 by affirming nonviolence not simply as an option for individuals, but also as a valid political option for states. Joseph Fahey notes that a similar process is happening in the liberal/mainstream Christian churches:

> While mainstream Christian bodies have long promulgated the just war model as their official teaching, the return in the late twentieth century to pacifism as a legitimate Christian witness is perhaps the most notable feature of contemporary Christian teaching on war and peace. . . .

Just War Criteria and Unitarian Universalism

Just War Criteria. In our prophetic critique of the government's justifications for war, we will of course draw on the just war criteria. These have a built-in familiarity and a rich set of interpretive traditions that make them extremely useful for this purpose, and public discourse about particular wars is likely to be carried on in just war language. Walter Wink argues even as a pacifist that the "just war criteria are indispensable in attempting to prevent or mitigate the hellishness of war." I noted earlier Wink's suggestion that they be called "violence reduction criteria" because that is their real goal. I want to extend this idea by arguing that we should turn the just war criteria around, and think of them not as a set of criteria for making the case for war, but rather as a list of reasons why war is not appropriate. The criterion of last resort, for example, tells us that war is unnecessary because there are always nonviolent alternatives. The criterion of proportionality tells us that war is wrong because it always causes more evil than it prevents. More than half of all war deaths during the twentieth century have been civilians—more than 50 million people, and this is beyond the incalculable physical and psychological suffering and property and cultural damage, both short and long term, that war always brings. In this light, using the criteria of right intention and probability of success to excuse this so-called "collateral damage" in the name of a larger good seems morally perverse. Approaching the just war criteria in this way can help us keep peace in the center of our ethical concerns.

Theological Principles. However, as helpful as the just war criteria may be for providing a basis for a critique of violence, we must remember that our real criteria—the true basis for our prophetic critique—are *our own theological principles.* In other words, our critique must be *our* critique, grounded in our Unitarian Universalist religious values and historical practices. I cannot develop these theological principles at length here, but I want to briefly identify several that are relevant to this task.

The Unitarian Universalist Principles

Unity. Unitarian Universalists affirm the basic unity of all existence. Beneath our individuality and our enormous diversity lies a profound relationality—an interdependent web—that connects us. This fundamental unity is what makes possible the idea of world community, a world in which there is no other to war against.

Love. Love is one of the deepest theological principles in our tradition. By affirming the value of love, we commit ourselves to creating relationships of compassion, respect, mutuality, and forgiveness. We commit ourselves to loving our neighbor, and to seeing everyone as our neighbor.

Worth of Persons. We affirm that all persons have inherent worth and dignity. Each of us, by virtue of our very humanness, is entitled to be treated with dignity and respect, and to have a meaningful and fulfilling life.

Freedom. Freedom is grounded in the inherent worth and dignity of every person. Because human beings are free moral agents, any form of coercion or violence is an assault on our very humanity. War is the product of human choices, and human beings have the moral capacity to make different choices.

Justice. Justice is manifested in the right ordering of human relationships. We have a religious obligation to create just communities and social structures, and an obligation to speak out against unjust practices and structures. War represents the breakdown of rightly ordered social relations.

Power. Power is always created and expressed in complex networks of human relationships. It can be exercised for good or evil; it can create or destroy, liberate or oppress. War is an expression of coercive and violent uses of power; peace and justice require cooperative forms of power. Power's ambiguous nature means that its use must be guided by our core values such as love and justice.

These are among the theological principles that should guide our prophetic critique of war. This means that in addition to applying the just war criteria, we must ask questions such as these: Does this military action promote or inhibit unity among all peoples? Does it express love and compassion toward our neighbors, or does it reflect fear and hate? Does it increase or restrict the possibilities for human freedom and fulfillment? Does it contribute to the creation of right relationships and just social structures, or does it harm these relationships? What kinds of power are being used, and by whom? These kinds of assessments will add power and depth to our prophetic practice. . . .

Clarity, Diversity, and Peace

I will close with a few brief observations. First, we need to be as clear and as theologically grounded as possible. Walter Wink puts this in blunt terms: "What the church needs most desperately is precisely . . . a clear-cut, unambiguous position." This is a good theological practice. Clarity will best serve individual members and congregations in their own discernment processes, and it will provide the most effective basis for prophetic critique. Any stance we may adopt as a denomination will be ineffective if it is simply a reaction to the current political situation. Instead, it must be a genuine expression of our Unitarian Universalist theological principles and religious values.

Second, we must honor the differences that exist among us. We will often disagree about our basic commitments around war and in our judgments about specific cases. This is not a reason to avoid the issue or to take so noncommittal a stance that we don't really say anything. But we need to be careful to welcome and honor those who hold dissenting views. We do well to remember that one of religious liberalism's core commitments is a principled open-mindedness that makes us suspicious of all claims of finality. We need not avoid taking strong stands, but we must always remain open to the possibility that we are wrong, or that circumstances we cannot now foresee may call for a different position at some point in the future.

Finally, we must avoid the dangers of political correctness. We do not have a very good record on this count. The ostracism suffered by those who held minority positions during World War I and the Vietnam War reflects an unfortunate streak of illiberal self-righteousness that runs deep, as any Republican in our midst can testify. I recognize the potential for this in my own position. By drawing on the commonalities between the just war and pacifist traditions and by emphasizing our Unitarian Universalist theological principles, I have tried to show that it is possible to formulate a position that can be endorsed by pacifists and just war advocates alike. My own proposal is surely not the only possibility for this. Yet a question that haunts me is whether our members who serve in the military would feel less welcome if my proposal were adopted as a denominational stance.

Whatever our individual views, we need to treat each other with compassion, respect, and love. . . . However inclusive our intentions and our language, we cannot eliminate all disagreement, nor should we try to do so. The very process of discussion through disagreement can help clarify our ideas and make us aware of the unintended consequences of our own words. At the same time, we need to remember that we belong to a shared religious tradition, and that our disagreements reflect our deeper levels of agreement—our shared theological principles and our shared commitment to peace.

Periodical and Internet Sources Bibliography

The following articles have been selected to supplement the diverse views presented in this chapter.

Chuck Baldwin	"Christian Pacifists Need to Correct Their Thinking," No Apologies, July 15, 2009. http://noapologies.ca.
Michael J. Baxter	"Just War and Pacifism: A 'Pacifist' Perspective in Seven Points," *Houston Catholic Worker*, May–June 2004.
Chuck Fager	"Rethinking Pacifism," *Christianity Today*, December 3, 2001.
Jim Foxvog	"Bible Pacifism: Christian Pacifism Is the Scriptural Position," Plow Creek Mennonite Church. www.plowcreek.org.
Travis Harvey	"The Crusade of Belmont's Religious Left," *Right Aisle Review*, May 5, 2009.
Daniel R. Heimbach	"The Problem of Universal Ethics for Christian Pacifism," *Journal of Faith and War*, September 18, 2009.
Logan Laituri	"Reinvigorating the Discourse on Just War and Pacifism," *God's Politics* (blog), February 2, 2010. http://blog.sojo.net.
Jim Moss	"Sunday Reading: Pacifism vs. Just War," *The Seminal* (blog), October 11, 2009. http://seminal.firedoglake.com.
Nick Nowalk	"Christian Pacifism and the Sermon on the Mount," *Harvard Ichthus*, October 20, 2009.
Mark D. Tooley	"Methodist Bishops Urge Surrender in Afghanistan," *FrontPage Magazine*, November 25, 2009.

OPPOSING VIEWPOINTS® SERIES

CHAPTER 2

How Do Other Religions View Pacifism?

Chapter Preface

Nonviolence, or ahimsa, is central to several religions including Hinduism, Buddhism, and Jainism. Ahimsa includes the practice of noninjury to living beings, compassion to all living creatures, vegetarianism, adoption of universal love, and other precepts of peace. According to Jayaram V on Hinduwebsite, ahimsa is based on the idea that "all living beings have their own destinies to fulfill, and are subject to the laws of karma and cycle of births and death. Killing a living being interferes with its destiny and spiritual progression." To kill another being, therefore, is harmful to the killer's own karma.

The most famous practitioner and exponent of ahimsa was the Indian Hindu leader Mahatma Gandhi. Gandhi was a key figure in the resistance movement against the British colonial occupation of India during the first part of the twentieth century. He was also an avid believer in nonviolence, noting that "my love for nonviolence is superior to that for every other thing—mundane or supramundane. It is equalled only by love for Truth, which is to me synonymous with nonviolence; through which and which alone I can see and reach Truth," as quoted by Ravindra Kumar in an October 14, 2007, article on NewsBlaze. Gandhi believed that nonviolence required a love for all humanity, including one's enemy. Thus, ahimsa was not merely a refraining from violence, but an active embrace of love.

The practical expression of ahimsa for Gandhi was Satyagraha, or soul-force. According to an article on the website of the Centre for Compassionate Social Change, "Satyagraha took the form of civil disobedience and non-cooperation with the law if it was believed to be unjust, and then facing the consequences." For example, in 1930 Gandhi led a 240-mile march to a coastal village, where he and followers gathered salt in defiance of a British salt law. This sparked a massive nonviolent resistance to the law, with one thousand individuals jailed. Actions like this undermined support for the British government at home and abroad, and eventually led to the independence of India in 1947.

Hinduism was central to Gandhi's practice of ahimsa and to his nonviolent resistance to injustice. At the same time, the practice of pacifism was inspiring in itself. Martin Luther King Jr., an American Christian minister, was led by Gandhi's example to adopt nonviolence in his own efforts to end discrimination and segregation in America. Different religious traditions around nonviolence, therefore, have influenced and sometimes contradicted each other. The following viewpoints look at various world religions and their attitudes toward pacifism.

VIEWPOINT 1

"The prevalent attitude among Muslims is that the revealed laws of God, properly interpreted and implemented, will inevitably lead to the ultimate desideratum: a just and peaceful world order."

Islam Has a Tradition of Peace

Asma Afsaruddin

Asma Afsaruddin is an associate professor of Arabic and Islamic studies at the University of Notre Dame. In the following viewpoint, she argues that Islam has a strong tradition of peace. She notes that the Qur'an and other Islamic texts see peace as an ideal. She says that pacifism, or nonresistance to injustice, is not part of the Islamic tradition but points out that Islamic thinking about war was an important influence on Christian just war thinking. She concludes that Islamic thinking about peace is an important resource for resolving international conflicts.

As you read, consider the following questions:

1. According to Afsaruddin, which is preferable in the Qur'an, the activist or the quietist striver in the way of God?

2. How does Afsaruddin define "pacificism"?
3. Who are Hugo Grotius, Francisco de Victorio, and Francisco Suárez?

It is commonly asserted that Islam does not endorse pacifism in the sense of an absolute and unconditional eschewal of violence, and there is considerable truth to this assertion. Mainstream Islamic teachings also do not endorse resorting to violence in the absence of extreme provocation. Violence as expressed in armed combat with a precisely defined enemy becomes permissible under certain conditions; during such combat, specific rules mandating humane and ethical conduct are in effect. Detailed as they are, Islamic military and social ethics still leave certain options ultimately to the conscience and interpretive abilities of the believer, allowing for a large measure of flexibility and adaptability to specific circumstances. . . .

Activism and Quietism

Some early pietistic [religiously devout] thinkers, for example, often in conscious opposition to other groups which urged a more activist approach to effect social and political change, chose to privilege certain Qur'anic verses and prophetic statements which advocate quietism and patient forbearance in the face of both personal trials and political tribulations. The Qur'an [the Muslim holy book] after all, equally endorses the activist and the quietist striver in the way of God (*al-mujahidun* and *al-sabirun* respectively). For example, Sura 16:110 states: "As for those who after persecution fled their homes and strove actively [*jahadu*] and were patient [*sabaru*] to the last, your Lord will be forgiving and merciful to them on the day when every soul will come pleading for itself." Another verse states: "We shall put you to the test until We know the active strivers [*al-mujahidin*] and the quietly forbearing [*al-sabirin*] among you." Quietist, nonviolent struggle is not to be confused with passivity, which when displayed in the face of grave oppression and injustice is clearly earmarked as immoral in the Qur'anic view.

The highly charged discourses that have grown up around the term *jihad* [Muslim religious war] obfuscate the fact that the term *sabr* (patience, forbearance) occurs far more often in the Qur'an than *qital* (fighting armed combat) as an element of *jihad*. Contrary to the recent statements of self-styled "experts", it is not those who engage in armed combat who earn unlimited divine approbation, according to the Qur'an. Rather, heavenly reward "without measure" and a lofty station in the next world are reserved only for those who cultivate "patience", understood as nonmilitant or quietist striving in the way of God.

The Qur'anic that has been construed to refer to the special status of the military martyr runs thus: "Do not think that those who were slain in the path of God are dead. They are alive and well provided for by their Lord." The exegetical and *hadith*[1] literature, however, makes clear that the phrase "slain in the path of God" is not restricted to those fallen in battle, but may be glossed in several ways. For example, a report found in an early work of *hadith*, 'Abd al-Razzaq's *al-Musannaf* from the eighth century C.E., states that there are four types of *shahada* or martyrdom for Muslims: the plague, parturition or childbirth, drowning, and a stomach ailment, with no mention of military activity (although a variant report includes it). The Qur'an in fact has no terms for "martyr" or "martyrdom". The term *shahid*, used later to refer to a martyr, occurs in the Qur'an only in the sense of a legal witness or eyewitness, and is applied both to God and humans. The development of the meaning of *shahid* in the sense of a martyr in extra-Qur'anic sources very likely owes something

1. The *hadith* are narrations originating from the words and actions of the Muslim prophet Muhammad.

The Role of War in the Islamic Tradition

According to the Koran [the Muslim holy book], war represents an "unwanted obligation" which has to be absolutely carried out with strict observance of particular humane and moral values and resorted only when it is inevitable. . . .

> . . . Each time they kindle the fire of war, Allah extinguishes it. They rush about the earth corrupting it. Allah does not love corrupters.

A closer examination of Prophet Muhammad's life reveals that war is a method resorted for defensive purposes only in unavoidable situations.

Harun Yahya,
"The Pacifism of Islam," February 10, 2004.
http://us1.harunyahya.com.

to Christian influence, since Christians had a well-developed concept of martyrdom by the time Muslims came into contact with them in the seventh century. . . .

Islam Evokes Peace

Muslims are known to assert proudly that the very name of their religion, *Islam*, is evocative of peace (in Arabic, *salam*, a cognate term) and that one of the names of the Almighty in Arabic is *al-Salam*. Sometimes the naïve assumption behind these assertions is that "proof" of this sort should be enough to convince the sceptic of the essentially peaceful nature of Islam. But, of course, peace does not devolve on its own; the establishment of a nonviolent social and world order requires conscious effort and constant vigilance, in addition to peaceful intent. Paradoxically, the maintenance of peace requires that those who would seek to subvert it must be resisted, sometimes violently, when peaceful means are exhausted.

The prevalent attitude among Muslims is that the revealed laws of God, properly interpreted and implemented, will inevitably lead to the ultimate desideratum: a just and peaceful world order. In general, the Islamic moral landscape has not been receptive to the idea of pursuing nonviolence as an ideological end in itself, severed from the requirement of fulfilling the conditions of social and political justice. Nonviolence, after all, can be (and has been) forcibly imposed by the strong on the weak to the detriment of the latter's rights and dignity. Thus pacifism, when defined as non-militancy under all circumstances and the unconditional avoidance of war, even in the face of violent aggression, may be regarded in specific situations as facilitating injustice and contributing to social instability.

The neologism "pacificism", on the other hand, more closely encapsulates traditional Islamic attitudes towards war and peace. Pacifism refers to a preference for peaceful conditions over war, but accepts that armed combat for defensive purposes may on occasion be necessary to advance the cause of peace. Conditional pacifism may be another way of referring to this position. In contrast, absolute pacifism harbours the possibility of acquiescing in injustice and evil, a moral infraction that is indefensible within the Islamic ethos. The Islamic principle of *hisba* (enjoining good and forbidding evil) instructs that refusal to resist wrong, even if only verbally, is a grave abdication of individual and collective moral responsibility.

Jihad and Just War

Battles fought for worldly (and in particular, political) reasons have been dubbed *jihad* by some Muslims, but by no means has there been consensus on this issue. Early *hadith* literature, like the *Musannaf* of 'Abd al-Razzaq, records the displeasure of pious Muslims at the military adventures of unscrupulous rulers. One *hadith* in the *Musannaf* specifically warns the pious not to join in the military campaigns of those "who fight seeking [the gains of] the world", otherwise they will forfeit their "portion in the hereafter". *Jus ad bellum* considerations of this sort (principles concerning when it is permissible to wage war) are to be found not so much in the legal corpus as in the literature that documents the dissent of the pious "laity", who often did not see eye to eye with the jurists. Very few Muslim rulers, in fact, have been deemed by the majority of Muslims as worthy of donning the Prophet's mantle and qualified to issue a call to *jihad* on behalf of the polity. Shi'ites have long held the view that in the absence of their infallible Imam [religious leader], the duty of *jihad* is in abeyance, a point of view similar to that of some Sunni modernists who are alarmed at the exploitation of this highly charged term by unscrupulous, self-appointed leaders. [Editor's Note: Shi'ite and Sunni are two important Muslim denominations.]

In the creation of a contemporary transnational legal discourse on war and peace, the substantial Islamic juridical corpus dealing with military ethics is not openly consulted by modern Western jurists. It has been suggested, however, that the introduction of *jus in bello* considerations (rules about proper conduct in war) into Western international law owes a debt to the Islamic legal heritage. Hugo Grotius, the seventeenth-century Dutch legal theorist credited with the formulation of statutes dealing with just conduct during war, was said to have been influenced by two Spanish jurists, Francisco de Victoria and Francisco Suárez. The latter in turn are said to have acknowledged drawing inspiration from Islamic legal thought prevalent in Muslim Spain. The beneficial cross-fertilisation of ideas between these two venerable legal cultures that this genealogy indicates suggests future beneficial consequences were such a process to continue.

Recent comparative studies of *jihad* and "just war" [the Christian doctrines discussing when war is justified] have, in fact, uncovered much common ground between them. Shared global concerns about the containment of violence and the amelioration of conditions which breed extremism mean that consensual international norms must be developed to deal with these questions effectively. Both Western and Islamic sources which contain rich repositories of moral thinking on these issues must be consulted to find legitimate, and ultimately, just solutions to these festering problems.

Viewpoint 2

> *"Islam is a violent, expansionary ideology that seeks the subjugation and destruction of other faiths, cultures and systems of government."*

Islam Embraces Violence

WorldNetDaily.com

WorldNetDaily (WND) is a conservative news website. In the following viewpoint, WND argues that Islam is inherently violent and that it is dedicated to attacking and conquering all non-Islamic nations. WND says Western governments are naïve when they claim that mainstream Islam is significantly different from radical militant Islam. Citing the book Religion of Peace?: Islam's War Against the World *by Gregory M. Davis, WND argues that Islam is an expansionary political ideology, more like Nazism or Communism than like Christianity or other religions.*

As you read, consider the following questions:

1. Why does WND say that Western leaders sent troops to the Middle East?
2. Into what two spheres does Davis say Islam divides the world?
3. What does Davis say is the aim of Islamic politics?

WorldNetDaily.com, "Is Islam Inherently Violent?" November 2, 2006. www.wnd.com.

It's *the* secret question in official Washington, D.C., in the Pentagon, and in the White House. It's the question that is so radioactive that most in government and the press dare not even pose it, let alone answer it:

Is Islam inherently violent and expansionist?

Not a Religion of Peace

In the days following 9/11 [September 11, 2001, terrorist attacks on the United States], President [George W.] Bush assured America and the world that Islam was a "religion of peace" and that the violent followers of Osama bin Laden had twisted the true Muslim faith. Acting on this belief, President Bush and other Western leaders sent troops to the Middle East [in 2003] in an effort to bring freedom and democracy to the Muslim world.

But what if this "understanding" of Islam is based not on fact, but instead on equal parts wishful thinking and Islamic deceit? It would mean that the entire War on Terror is based on a faulty—and increasingly deadly—premise.

In a disturbing but thoroughly researched new book, *Religion of Peace?: Islam's War Against the World*, author and filmmaker Gregory M. Davis rebuts the notion that Islam is a great faith in desperate need of a reformation. Instead, he exposes it as a form of totalitarianism, a belief system that orders its adherents not to baptize all nations, but to conquer and subdue them. Islamic law's governance of every aspect of religious, political and personal action has far more in common with Nazism than with the tenets of Christianity or Judaism.

Perpetual Combat

Davis details how Islamic thought divides the world into two spheres locked in perpetual combat: There's Dar al-Islam ("House of Islam," where Islamic law predominates), and Dar al-harb ("House of War," the rest of the world). This concise

The Koran Is Violent

If you say that Islam is a violent faith, you are accused of being anti-Islam and you are propagating "Islamophobia."

There are more than one billion Muslims around the world, and I'm one of them. We are told that the Koran [the Muslim holy book] is the "word of God." When you read the Koran, however—which over 90% of all Muslims have never read, according to a survey by Bielefeld University in Germany, and if they ever do, either they do not understand its archaic language or they do not ponder on what it says—you find out that it is full of passages that incite to hatred, killing, and discriminate against women.

Sami Alrabaa, "Is Islam a Violent Faith? Violence, Hatred and Discrimination in the Koran," Family Security Matters, January, 16, 2009. www.familysecuritymatters.org.

yet thorough book leaves no doubt as to why most of the world's modern conflicts are connected to Islam—and calls into question why Western elites refuse to acknowledge Islam's violent nature.

Virtually every contemporary Western leader has expressed the view that Islam is a peaceful religion and that those who commit violence in its name are fanatics who misinterpret its tenets. This widely circulated claim is false, says Davis.

As the author and filmmaker wrote in WND [WorldNet Daily] recently:

> The mistake Westerners make when they think about Islam is that they impose their own views of religion onto something decidedly outside Western tradition. Because violence

> done in the name of God is "extreme" from a Western/Christian point of view, they imagine that it must be so from an Islamic one. But unlike Christianity, which recognizes a separate sphere for secular politics ("Render unto Caesar what is Caesar's and unto God what is God's"), Islam has never distinguished between faith and power. While Christianity is doctrinally concerned primarily with the salvation of souls, Islam seeks to remake the world in its image. According to orthodox Islam, Sharia law—the codified commandments of the Quran [the Muslim holy book] and precedents of the Prophet Muhammad—is the only legitimate basis of government. Islam is in fact an expansionary social and political system more akin to National Socialism and Communism than any "religion" familiar to Westerners. Islamic politics is inevitably an all-or-nothing affair in which the stakes are salvation or damnation and the aim is not to beat one's opponent at the polls but to destroy him—literally as well as politically.

Davis received his PhD in political science from Stanford University and is managing director of Quixotic Media and producer of the feature documentary, *Islam: What the West Needs to Know.*

Relying primarily on Islam's own sources, *Religion of Peace?: Islam's War Against the World* demonstrates that Islam is a violent, expansionary ideology that seeks the subjugation and destruction of other faiths, cultures and systems of government. Further, it shows that the jihadis [Islamic militants] that Westerners have been indoctrinated to believe are extremists, are actually in the mainstream.

Religion of Peace?: Islam's War Against the World is a powerful and jarring wake-up call to all civilized nations—and one they ignore at their peril.

Viewpoint 3

> *"Torah's essential purpose is peace. . . . But peace, we are taught, must be continually sought—it will not come naturally to us."*

Judaism Has a Tradition of Nonviolence

Brant Rosen

Brant Rosen is the rabbi at the Jewish Reconstructionist Congregation in Evanston, Illinois. In the following viewpoint, he notes that Judaism is not a pacifist tradition. However, he argues that peace is central to the Jewish religion, which teaches that violence is a form of moral pollution. He adds that for a victimized people like the Jews, nonviolence is an especially difficult path. However, he concludes that Jews are enjoined to seek peace, and he argues that nonviolence is ultimately the best path for Jews, for Israel, and for the world.

As you read, consider the following questions:

1. What does Rosen say is ignored during the annual Martin Luther King Jr. celebrations?

Brant Rosen, "Judaism as Nonviolence: A Sermon for Rosh Hashanah," rabbirant.com, September 21, 2009.

2. Those who deny pacifist values in Jewish tradition often point to what, according to Rosen?
3. What does Rosen believe is the result of Israel's use of overwhelming military power to solve political problems?

During my Rosh Hashanah sermon, I asked the following questions:

> Is there a place in Judaism for pacifism? Is it in fact possible—or desirable—as a Jew, to walk the path of nonviolence? . . .

Judaism Is Not Pacifist

Whenever Jewish tradition's views on war and peace are being discussed, you'll often hear some version of this statement: "Judaism is not a pacifist religion." I've made this claim myself on more than one occasion. In fact, before I begin this year's [2009's] sermon, I'd like to read you an excerpt from the sermon I gave on Rosh Hashanah [the Jewish New Year] 2003. If you think back on that time, you'll remember: 9/11 [September 11, 2001, terrorist attacks on the United States] was still fresh on our souls, the war with Iraq had begun a few months earlier, and I had decided to make a sharp statement against our nation's increasingly militaristic foreign policy.

I'll quote from my sermon verbatim:

> I suppose the place to start is to point out that Judaism is not a pacifist tradition and it never has been. From its Israelite origins until present day, Jewish tradition has viewed war as something that is occasionally permitted and in some circumstances, even necessary.

Now, I'm not here to retract this statement. But I would like to explore it a bit more deeply. I'd like to revisit this comment because I'm increasingly struck by how easily Jews stereotype pacifism—how we tend to set it up as a kind of overidealistic straw horse that we can easily knock aside. And in the end, I'm not sure that's such a good thing. Because when we dismiss the work of nonviolence, I fear that we end up becoming jaded and cynical over the very prospect of peace itself.

It's now six years since I've given that sermon, but I believe the issue is germane as ever. As 2009 draws to a close, our country is still engaged in two foreign wars, neither of which show any sign of ending soon. Though our new administration [under President Barack Obama] is now making what I consider to be valiant attempts at diplomacy, the challenges are daunting and the prospects for failure are terrifying, particularly in the Middle East. In so many ways, the threat—and the tragedy—of war is still very much a part of our times.

And yet perhaps it ever was thus. It would be foolish to deny that war has been an indelible aspect of human history from time immemorial. Though most of us consider peacemaking to be an important value, it's a value we seldom honor all that well. War is what we know. It's what we've always known. The pursuit of nonviolence is also a part of our history, certainly, and we love to invoke it from time to time—but I'd say we rarely stop to consider it seriously. When push comes to shove, most of us consider pacifism at best to be a lovely, if somewhat naïve little dream. We're great at paying it lip service, but how often do we seriously consider its meaning? How often do we really, truly attempt to walk the walk?

Martin Luther King Jr.'s Commitment to Nonviolence

The way we commemorate the legacy of Dr. Martin Luther King Jr. [MLK] is a prime example of this phenomenon. Truly, there are few more beloved and celebrated contemporary national heroes than Martin Luther King. Indeed, we've devoted a national holiday to his memory and he is taught in our schools nearly as much as our country's Founding Fathers. But rarely during our annual MLK celebrations do we explore how his sophisticated and challenging philosophy of nonviolence informed the struggle for civil rights in our country.

On MLK day, we'll inevitably hear his "I Have a Dream" speech quoted repeatedly. But I doubt our nation would ever invoke—let alone seriously conisder—a quote such as this, which he wrote in an article shortly before he was assassinated:

> I'm committed to nonviolence absolutely. I'm just not going to kill anybody, whether it's in Vietnam or here. I'm not going to burn down any building. If nonviolent protest fails this summer, I will continue to preach it and teach it . . . I plan to stand by nonviolence because I have found it to be a philosophy of life that regulates not only my dealings in the struggle for racial justice, but also my dealings with people, with my own self. I will still be faithful to nonviolence.

So as a Jew who is also deeply inspired by teachings such as this—as someone who struggles to remain faithful to these kinds of values, I ask: Is there a place in Judaism for pacifism? Is it in fact possible—or desirable—as a Jew, to walk the path of nonviolence?

I'd like to start out by clarifying our terms. Up until now I've been using the terms "pacifism" and "nonviolence" somewhat interchangeably, but I should be more precise. Generally speaking, the term "pacifism" refers to a psychological state or a state of mind. Pacifism is a value, an ideal—a moral belief that rejects war and violence as a means for resolving conflict.

Nonviolence, on the other hand, is a way of life. I think one of the biggest misconceptions about nonviolence is that [it] is essentially passive. Perhaps this is because the term defines itself by what it isn't. In fact, nonviolence is inherently *activist*. In truth, it is actually as active as violence itself inasmuch as they are both forms of persuasion. They both seek to change or transform the status quo. Nonviolence is essentially rooted in essentially a pragmatic approach—but it is committed to resolving conflicts *peacefully*. It is based on the core belief that is eminently practical in nature: that nonviolence is simply more effective than violence. That war *does not work.*

Judaism and Peace

This idea is, in fact, deeply embedded in Judaism. Through the maze of Jewish tradition's myriad of confusing and often seemingly contradictory commandments, we are repeatedly reminded that Torah's essential purpose is peace. Every time we return the Torah scroll to the ark we do so with these Biblical words, "Torah is a Tree of Life . . . all its ways are ways of peace." The Talmud (Chapter Gittin) drives this idea home in a very straightforward manner: "The *whole* of Torah is for the purpose of promoting peace."

But peace, we are taught, must be continually sought—it will not come naturally to us. In Psalm 34, another important part of our liturgy, we read "Seek peace and pursue it." In Pirkei Avot [a compilation of rabbinical teachings], Rabbi Hillel teaches, "Be students of Aaron: love peace and pursue peace." Now these are lovely words, but they are more than just moral platitudes. Over and over in our tradition we are taught that peace is not simply a value to be cherished—it is a goal to be actively sought out. Peace will not, it cannot come to us all by itself. Peace will only come to us if we ourselves see fit to work for it. Otherwise, war and bloodshed will continue to be our default status quo.

Those who deny pacifist values in Jewish tradition often point to its complex laws of warfare. And it's true: Jewish law spends a great deal of time discussing when we are and aren't justified in going to war. In *halacha* [Jewish religious law], this is embodied by the concept of *Milchemet Mitzvah* (or a "commanded war.") Under this category are two instances in which we are literally obliged to go to war. One is the commandment to fight the so-called seven pagan nations that occupied the ancient Land of Israel as well as the enemy tribe known as the Amalekites. What do we make of this commandment today? Many Jewish commentators suggest that this category belongs to an ancient Near Eastern setting that is simply no more. That is to say, since these nations no longer exist, this particular commandment is now null and void.

However, the rabbis also applied the concept of *Milchemet Mitzvah* to any war of self-defense. A famous law from the Talmud rules that one is commanded to kill a pursuer ("*rodef*") who is threatening your life. So too are nations given the responsibility to defend themselves against [those] who attack them. However—and this is a big however—before we go to war, we are commanded to seek peace at all costs—to exhaust every possibility for peaceful resolutions to conflict.

That is because war and violence have an irrevocable impact on our lives and on our world. Another classic Jewish teaching, the Mekhilta of Rabbi Ishmael, teaches: "When an arrow leaves the hand of a warrior he cannot take it back." From this we learn that once we resort to war, we unleash a myriad of consequences that we can neither control nor reverse.

Violence as Moral Pollution

Jewish tradition also teaches us that violence is a form of moral pollution that stains our world indelibly. The most famous example of this occurs in Genesis. After Cain kills Abel, God says to him, "Your brother's blood cries out to me from the ground. Therefore, you shall be more cursed than the ground, which opened its mouth to receive your brother's blood from your hand." I understand this to mean that . . . violence does not only cause personal suffering and loss—it transforms our collective world forever.

Indeed, war has a way of unleashing hatred into the world in a profound and indelible manner. It invariably creates cycles of violence that compound pain and division—and by so doing these cycles render the prospect of peace infinitely more difficult, if not impossible. This is the tragic irony of war: It is virtually always justified in terms of self-defense. But inevitably, war creates an endless reality of its own in which each side ends up defining the other in terms of its latest attack.

An orthodox rabbinic colleague once put it this way to me: "According to Jewish law, a *Milchemet Mitzvah*—a commanded war—is a war of self-defense. That essentially means that war is always justified or war is never justified." With all due respect to "just war" theory, I tend to agree with my colleague. It often seems so very ironic that war, the most extreme and horrific manifestation of human violence, also tends to be the easiest for us to excuse, rationalize and explain away. But those who have fought in wars will attest that there is nothing moral or good about them. According to international law, there are "legal" and "illegal" ways of waging them, but most who actually see the field of battle report that in the fog of war, the fine points of battlefield morality invariably become blurred, often to the point of meaninglessness.

Though I respect the opinions of those who feel otherwise, I have personally come to believe that the shades of gray are merely a delusion. At the end of the day we will have to choose: Do we believe that war is an acceptable way to settle conflicts, or do we believe that it is simply unacceptable? And if our answer is the latter, then what are we prepared to do about it?

I know that this is an enormously difficult issue for Jews in particular. I think there is a good reason why you rarely hear the words "Judaism" and "pacifism" mentioned together—and I'm not sure it ultimately has anything to do with religious ideology. We Jews have been a historically vulnerable people. We've been the literal object of violence for centuries. And of course there is no getting around it: to be a Jew today means to live in traumatic aftermath of the Holocaust—to know all too painfully the costs of not being able to physically defend ourselves. I know this is why Israel represents what it does for so many Jews. In a very deep way, it represents our Jewish empowerment after having been so vulnerable for so long—and especially following the most tragically powerless chapters in our history. For the first time in centuries, we now have their own nation with their own army, prepared and ready to defend the security of the Jewish people.

Israel and Violence

But now, sixty years after the founding of Israel, it is well worth asking: Has Israel solved what Theodor Herzl [an Austro-Hungarian Jewish journalist] called "the Jewish problem"? When Herzl developed political Zionism [the political campaign for a Jewish state], he truly believed that the founding of a Jewish state would end anti-Semitism once and for all. And yet, for all its formidable, state-of-the-art military might, Israel has found neither safety nor security. This is the great tragic irony of our time: The place in the world where the Jewish people is ostensibly the most powerful is the place where endless war has become its lot. Of course, we could analyze the history of the Israel-Palestinian conflict and debate its causes as long as we like, but again, the larger question remains: Has Israel's military power brought the Jewish people the peace and stability for which we have prayed for so long?

Many of you know that I speak out very publicly when I believe Israel uses its power in a manner that I consider oppressive—and I know it is difficult for many in the Jewish community to hear me criticize Israel in such a public way. There will be time to debate into the specifics of the Mideast conflict—and as a congregation we should. We should share openly and honestly our beliefs, our concerns and our fear over this painful and challenging and tragic situation. But for now I will only say that when I speak out, please know I do it as a matter of personal conscience. I do so out of a deep and

The First Tale of Nonviolent Civil Disobedience

Over its long history, how has the Jewish people viewed violence and nonviolence as approaches to tikkun olam, social change in the service of the healing of the world? (The literal phrase "tikkun olam" has been used in that sense only recently, but the vision that one major purpose of Jewish peoplehood is to achieve justice, peace, and ecological wholeness is a very old vision.)

If we look back at the history of biblical Israel, there are two very important strands in it, both of which we need to learn from and wrestle with. One is the strand of constant willingness to challenge and disobey arrogant power, whether it's located in Pharaoh or it's located in a Jewish king. The other is the strand of willingness to use violence—sometimes hyper-violence—to advance the Jewish vision of a decent society.

Let us . . . take up the strand of resistance to unaccountable power. The story of Shifrah and Puah—the midwives who refused to obey Pharaoh's order to murder Hebrew boy–babies—is perhaps the first tale of nonviolent civil disobedience in world literature.

Arthur O. Waskow,
"Sword and Plowshare as Tools of Tikkun Olam: Violence & Nonviolence in Jewish Thought & Action,"
The Shalom Center, October 2, 2007.
www.theshalomcenter.org.

abiding love for the Jewish people. And I do so out [of] my belief that the use of overwhelming military power to solve political problems is not making Israel more secure, but precisely the opposite.

Frankly, I believe the same thing about the US and our own militarized foreign policy as well. Believe me, I have no illusions about the so-called military-industrial complex (or as it's often referred to today: the "corporate-industrial complex.") This is how the world works. War today is big business. It has been observed that war will be with us as long as there are those who can make good money off of it. I'm not so naïve as to say we are going to fundamentally turn around the scourge of war from our midst. But I do also know that history is replete with examples in which nonviolence has stared down the advocates of war and violence and have succeeded. It is not just a naïve dream. People such as [Indian revolutionary Mahatma] Gandhi and King and [South African leader Nelson] Mandela are the most prominent examples of this, but there are many, many more heroes who have changed the world in large and small ways through the path of nonviolence.

Nonviolence Can Bring Change

And for those who scoff that ivory tower morals can never change the scheme of things, I submit the words of Václav Havel, the Czech essayist and playwright who helped to bring down an oppressive regime [of communism] and eventually became president:

> Even a purely moral act that has no hope of any immediate and visible political effect can gradually and indirectly, over time, gain in political significance.

Does Judaism believe in nonviolence? For me, at least, it comes down to this: I believe that our spiritual tradition teaches that the pursuit of peace is an absolutely sacrosanct value; that this is an ideal that we are commanded to put into action; and that it does indeed have the power to change the world. I also know that it is enormously challenging to belong to people with a legacy of victimization—and remain committed to a path of nonviolence. But today, in this age of unprecedented Jewish power, I also believe in my heart that physical power will not ultimately bring us the security that we seek. And in my darkest moments, I fear that, God forbid, it could even prove our downfall.

As I mentioned, . . . Rosh Hashanah is a time in which we publicly acknowledge the limits of human power—the one time of year in which we literally bow to the ground to a Power that ultimately transcends us all. I've often believed that in its way, this is an ironically empowering moment. For it's only when we affirm the limits of our own power that we understand what we are truly capable of in this world. I hope this Rosh Hashanah, we can begin to discover the true source of our power: not by wielding it against others, but by choosing another means of affecting change in the world: the path of nonviolence, which is just as effective, but infinitely more sacred.

I hope it is a path we can search for and struggle toward together. May it make a difference in our lives and world—and may we all live to see that day.

VIEWPOINT 4

> *"If Jewish violence against [Adolf] Hitler was right, then violence is not always and everywhere wrong."*

Jewish History Shows Absolute Pacifism Is Wrong

David B. Kopel

David B. Kopel is an author and an attorney. He is research director of the Independence Institute and associate policy analyst at the Cato Institute. In the following viewpoint, he argues that, contrary to pacifist teachings, Jews were morally right to actively resist German violence during the Holocaust. He says that violence by Jews against the Nazis saved lives and earned the Jews respect and some outside help. He concludes that the best way to prevent genocides is to arm threatened populations.

As you read, consider the following questions:

1. According to Kopel, what was the only extermination camp put out of business early, and where was it located?
2. According to Kopel, how did Jewish resistance in the Warsaw ghetto change Western attitudes toward Jews?

3. What evidence does Kopel provide that democracy and a free press are not guarantees against genocide?

This [viewpoint] examines the record of violent Jewish resistance to the Holocaust. It suggests that Jewish resistance was extensive, and succeeded in saving many lives. The record also explains that a key impediment to even more effective resistance was the lack of firearms, as well as Jewish unfamiliarity with arms during the pre-war years. The [viewpoint] dispels the myth of Jewish passivity during the Holocaust, and the myth that courageous civilians with firearms are helpless against a powerful, genocidal tyranny.

Violent Resistance Was Justified

When we examine the record of Jews and the Holocaust, it is necessary to tell the story of some people who behaved very wickedly. Although their violations may have been the result of the great stresses and pressures of the time, it cannot be denied that these people performed terribly evil acts. If you, reader, are a pacifist, then you must not apply these words to the Nazis alone. For a committed pacifist, these words must also apply to the Jews who used violence to resist the Holocaust. If violence—especially deadly violence—is always and everywhere immoral, then the Jews who violently resisted [German dictator Adolf] Hitler acted immorally. Rather than killing the extermination camp guards at Sobibor, the Jews should have allowed themselves to be slaughtered. Rather than waging partisan warfare in the woods of Eastern Europe, the Jews should not have picked up guns.

If you can honestly say that the story of Jewish resistance to Hitler is horrific rather than honorable, if you sincerely believe that the Jews did the wrong thing when they fought back, then you may wear the title of a consistent pacifist. If, on the other hand, you think that the Jews were not blameworthy for what they did, then you are not a complete pacifist. If Jewish violence against Hitler was right, then violence is not always and everywhere wrong.

Different people may, of course, disagree about the prudence or the appropriateness of violence in different circumstances—but the disagreement is about circumstances. The nature of disagreement recognizes that, in at least some circumstances, violence is not wrongful. Indeed, the failure to use violence may itself be wrongful.

Let us now examine the record of defensive Jewish violence during the Holocaust.

Despite pleas from Jewish organizations, the Allies never bombed the train tracks leading to the extermination camps. Historians still argue about whether the Allied decision was correct; some argue that the missions were too dangerous, that the bombers were needed elsewhere, or that the tracks could have been quickly repaired. Whatever the merits of the Allied refusal, the fact remains that every extermination camp in Nazi Europe continued operating until Allied ground forces advanced to the general area. There was never any offensive aimed specifically at an extermination camp.

The Violence at Sobibor

The one camp that was put out of business early was the Sobibor extermination camp in Poland. As detailed in the book and movie *Escape from Sobibor*, and in memoirs of the survivors, Sobibor was a horribly efficient camp, gassing thousands of people per day. The camp was run by Germans, with the assistance of several dozen Ukrainian guards. Much of the day-to-day work of the camp, such as carpentry, sewing uniforms, and processing the dead bodies, was performed by a crew of specially selected Jews, who performed the work in exchange for, temporarily, being allowed to live.

When some Soviet Jewish prisoners of war [POWs] were brought into the camp, the POWs began organizing an escape.

Jewish Lives Taken in the Holocaust

Country	Initial Jewish Population	Estimated % Killed	Estimated Killed	Number of Survivors
Poland	3,300,000	91%	3,000,000	300,000
USSR	3,020,000	36%	1,100,000	1,920,000
Hungary	800,000	74%	596,000	204,000
Germany	566,000	36%	200,000	366,000
France	350,000	22%	77,320	272,680
Romania	342,000	84%	287,000	55,000
Austria	185,000	35%	65,000	120,000
Lithuania	168,000	85%	143,000	25,000
Netherlands	140,000	71%	100,000	40,000
Bohemia Moravia	118,310	60%	71,150	47,160
Latvia	95,000	84%	80,000	15,000
Slovakia	88,950	80%	71,000	17,950
Yugoslavia	78,000	81%	63,300	14,700
Greece	77,380	87%	67,000	10,380
Belgium	65,700	45%	28,900	36,800
Italy	44,500	17%	7,680	36,820
Bulgaria	50,000	0%		50,000
Denmark	7,800	.8%	60	7,740
Estonia	4,500	44%	2,000	2,500
Luxembourg	3,500	55%	1,950	1,550
Finland	2,000	.03%	7	1,993
Norway	1,700	45%	762	938
Total	9,508,340	63%	5,962,129	3,546,211

TAKEN FROM: *History Place*, "Statistics of the Holocaust," n.d., www.historyplace.com.

Although there was a constant danger that Jewish spies, in exchange for favored treatment, might reveal the plans to the Nazis, the plan went forward. With crude improvised weapons, the inmates hurriedly killed a few Nazi officers, and obtained the keys to the camp armory.

In the wild battle that ensued, 600 prisoners tried to flee; about 400 of them escaped the camp boundaries, and about half of them survived the land mine field around the camp. More escapees were caught later, but a band of 60 men and women, led by the Soviet officer Alexander Pechersky, made contact with the Soviet partisans. Ten SS [Nazi] troops were killed, and one was wounded. Thirty-eight Ukrainian guards were killed or wounded, while forty Ukrainian guards took the opportunity to desert.

Four days after the revolt, a special German unit destroyed the Sobibor camp completely, to attempt to keep the revolt a secret. A death camp which had already murdered six hundred thousand people was put out of operation forever.

"Violence never solves anything" is one of the platitudes which American schoolchildren are told over and over. Sobibor shows that the platitude is a deadly falsehood. Violence solved Sobibor. The solution to Hitler's Final Solution was violence—the violent destruction of the Nazi regime. The Jews at Sobibor did their part.

Sobibor was the site of the greatest violent revolt, but it was not the only one. Jews rose up at four other extermination camps and eighteen forced labor camps or death camps. Of these revolts, the August 1943 revolt of 700 inmates at Treblinka was the most successful. The prisoners used improvised explosive to set fires, and improvised knives to kill guards. The huge fire disabled much of Treblinka. About 150 to 200 prisoners escaped, and of them, a dozen survived until the end of the war. None would have survived had they remained passive, and all seven hundred died with honor.

Of all the German concentration and extermination camps that were built all over Europe, it was *only* the Jewish camps where there were revolts. (Except for a rebellion by Soviet prisoners of war at the Ebensee camp.)

The Warsaw Ghetto

Before the war, about ten percent of Poland's population was Jewish. In the middle ages, Poland had been a welcoming, tolerant, and free nation, and many Jews emigrated there. But when Poland regained its independence in 1919 thanks to the

Versailles Treaty [after World War I], the nation quickly degenerated into a military dictatorship which encouraged anti-Semitism.

In Poland, as in other Eastern European areas under Nazi military rule, all the Jews in a city would be ordered to move into a walled ghetto. Movement in and out of the ghetto was very strictly controlled. The Germans would set up a *Judenrät* of collaborationist Jews to run the ghetto, and to punish any attempts at rebellion. The *Judenrät* received special privileges from the Nazis. Often, the *Judenrät* was assured that as long as the ghetto worked hard to produce factory goods for the Germans, the ghetto would be allowed to survive.

Eventually, the Germans would begin deporting large numbers of people from the ghetto—ostensibly for resettlement in labor camps, but almost always for extermination. The *Judenrät* would be required to select the Jews to be deported. Eventually, the whole ghetto would be depopulated, and the area would be declared *Judenrein* (Jew-free).

In Warsaw, the large prewar Jewish population was initially supplemented by large numbers of Jews who were shipped in from other cities. The Jews were forced to live on starvation rations, and many thousands in the ghetto died from starvation or contagious disease. The Germans eventually cut the size of the ghetto in half, consolidating the survivors into extremely crowded conditions. Deportations to the death camps continued to depopulate the ghetto.

In late 1942, Emmanuel Ringelblum, the well-educated author of a diary about life in the Warsaw ghetto, wrote:

> Whomever you talk to, you hear the same cry: The resettlement never should have been permitted. We should have run into the street, set fire to everything in sight, have torn down the walls, and escaped to the Other Side. The Germans would have taken their revenge. It would have cost tens of thousands of lives, but not 300,000. Now we are ashamed of ourselves, disgraced in our own eyes, and in the

> eyes of the world, where our docility has earned us nothing. This must not be repeated now. We must put up a resistance, defend ourselves against the enemy, man and child.

Resistance Sent a Powerful Message

On January 18, 1943, the Germans rounded up seven thousand Jews and sent them to the extermination camp at Treblinka; they killed six hundred more Jews right in Warsaw. But on that day, an uprising began. In the beginning, the Jewish fighting organization had about 600 volunteers; the Jewish military association had about 400, and there were thousands more in spontaneous small groups. The Jews had only ten handguns, but the Germans did not realize how under-armed the Jewish fighters were.

After four days of fighting, the Germans on January 21 pulled back from the ghetto, to organize better. Another diary written in the Warsaw ghetto exulted:

> In the four days of fighting we had made up for the same of Jewish passivity in the first extermination action of July, 1942.
>
> Not only the Germans were shocked by the unexpected resistance, Jews too were astonished. They could not imagine until then that the beaten, exhausted victims could rise against a mighty enemy who had conquered all of Europe. Many Jews who were in the streets of Warsaw during the fighting refused to believe that on Zamenhof and Mila Streets Jewish boys and girls had attacked Germans. The large-scale fighting which followed convinced all that it was possible. . . .

The Warsaw Jews knew they had almost no chance of survival. They decided that it was better to die fighting than to die in a gas chamber. It was better to kill at least some of the killers, than to let them massacre Jews with impunity. Ringelblum wrote, "We took stock of our position and saw that this was a struggle between a fly and an elephant. But our national dignity dictated to us that the Jews must offer resistance and not allow themselves to be led wantonly to slaughter."

Warsaw was the first mass civilian uprising against the Nazis anywhere in Europe. On April 23, the Jewish commander, 25-year-old Mordechai Anielewicz, had written, "I have a feeling that great things are happening, that what we have undertaken is of tremendous significance." He was right.

As the West learned about the Warsaw Revolt, the Western media began to change its attitude towards Jews. "They concluded that the Jews had earned the right to be regarded not as supplicants, but as allies." An article in *Harper's* explained, "As the British press was the first to admit, the Jews now have a new and different claim for consideration, a claim not of passive victims, but of active allies and partners who have fought the common enemy." . . .

Jews Fight in Disproportionate Numbers

In 1942–43, Jews constituted half of all the partisans [irregular fighters against the Nazis] in Poland. Overall, about thirty thousand Jewish partisans fought in Eastern Europe. There were armed revolts in over forty different ghettos, mostly in Eastern Poland.

In other parts of Europe, Jews likewise joined the resistance at much higher rates than the rest of the population. Unlike in Eastern Europe, though, Jews were generally able to participate as individuals in the national resistance, rather than having to fight in separate units.

For example, in France, Jews amounted to [less] than one percent of French population, but comprised about 15–20 percent of the French Resistance.

In Greece too, Jews were disproportionately involved in the resistance. In Thessaly, a Jewish partisan unit in the mountains was led by the septuagenarian Rabbi Moshe Pesah, who carried his own rifle. The Athenian Jew Jacques Costis led the team which demolished the Gorgopotamos Bridge, thereby breaking the link between the mainland and Peloponnesian Peninsula, and interfering with the delivery of supplies to [Erwin] Rommel's Afrika Korps [fighting in North Africa].

Jews Needed Arms

Although Jews resisted Hitler more so than any other group behind Nazi lines, the majority of Jews did not engage in armed resistance. Many Jews failed to realize until too [late] that Hitler was different from their previous enemies. Hitler really did mean to wipe out all the Jews, not merely to exploit them economically, to move them to new locations, or to kill only some of them.

Another huge barrier to resistance was that the Jews were unarmed. Except in the Zionist [a political movement in favor of the establishment of a Jewish state] self-defense units, there was no gun culture among most of Europe's Jews. Prewar Poland, the home of the largest number of Jews who were murdered, was a poorly armed nation. The anti-Semitic government was hostile to gun ownership by workers.

Unlike all the other undergrounds in Europe, the Jewish partisans received no weapons from the Allies. Holocaust scholar Nechama Tec summarizes: "As regards resistance, in practical terms, the Allies had virtually no interest in the Jews. This indifference translated into a rejection of all known Jewish pleas, including those requesting arms and ammunition. It goes without saying that the Jews experienced a chronic arms shortage." (The U.S. and Britain did supply arms to the French Resistance, which had a large number of Jews. The Americans and British also supplied arms to the Soviet Union, which in turn supplied some arms to Soviet partisan units, and some of the Soviet units included Jews.)

According to Emmanuel Ringelbaum's history of the Warsaw ghetto, "We state firmly that had the responsible Polish authorities extended moral support and helped us with arms, the Germans would have had to pay for the sea of Jewish blood shed in July, August, and September 1942," as Jews were deported to Treblinka.

Writes the Holocaust historian Abram L. Sachar:

> The indispensable need, of course, was arms. As soon as some Jews, even in the camps themselves, obtained possession of a weapon, however pathetically inadequate—a rifle, an ax, a sewer cover, a homemade bomb—they used it and often took Nazis with them to death.

Thus, writes Sachar, "the difference between resistance and submission depended very largely upon who was in possession of the arms that back up the will to do or die."

The Warsaw ghetto commander, Mordechai Anielewicz, believed that:

> We should have trained the youth in use of live and cold ammunition. We should have raised them in a spirit of revenge against the greatest enemy of the Jews, of all mankind, and of all times. . . .

In 1967, the International Society for the Prevention of Crime held a Congress in Paris on the prevention of genocide. The Congress concluded that

> defensive measures are the most effective means for the prevention of genocide. Not all aggression is criminal. A defense reaction is for the human race what the wind is for navigation—the result depends on the direction. The most moral violence is that used in legitimate self-defense, the most sacred judicial institution.

No More Genocide

Today, almost every religious group in the world has deplored the Holocaust. The only significant exceptions are in the Muslim world; Hitler's admirers at the time included the Grand Mufti of Jerusalem (the mentor of Yasser Arafat) and the 1943 founders of the Ba'ath Party in Iraq and Syria.

There is a difference, though, between retrospectively deploring the Holocaust, and taking action to prevent future genocides. It is nice for human rights groups to encourage democracy and a free press, but neither are guarantees against genocide. Adolf Hitler obtained power legally in Weimar Germany, a democratic nation with a free press. It is also nice for religious groups to encourage war crimes trials for people who perpetrate genocide. The trials of Serbian and Rwandan mass murderers may have some deterrent effect.

The historical record shows that, almost without exception, genocide is preceded by a very careful government program that disarms the future victims of genocide. Genocide is almost never attempted against an armed population. Armenia, Rwanda, Bosnia, China, Guatemala, Cambodia, Uganda, the Soviet Union, the Sudan, and Nazi Europe are among the places where genocidal tyrants made very sure that the victim populations were as disarmed as possible; only after disarmament did genocide begin. However much gun prohibition activists may scoff at the idea of civilian resistance to genocide, it is worth remembering that the governments which carry out genocide take the idea of armed civilians quite seriously.

Armed Jews (or armed Cambodians, or Chinese, or other genocide victims) would not necessarily be able to fight open-field battles against standing armies. But to deter genocide, an armed population does not have to fight such battles.

The kind of people who specialize in perpetrating genocide are bullies. How many bullies are willing to take a chance of getting shot by the intended victim? If potential massacre victims can plausibly threaten to harm at least a few of their attackers, then the calculus of the attackers may change dramatically.

Besides directly facilitating the ability of armed soldiers to control unarmed civilian genocide victims, there is a second way in which disarmament promotes genocide. As the American founder Joel Barlow wrote, "Disarmament palsies the hand and brutalizes the mind: an habitual disuse of physical force totally destroys the moral; and men lose at once the power of protecting themselves, and of discerning the cause of their oppression."

If every family in the world owned a good-quality rifle and an ample supply of ammunition, genocide would be greatly reduced, and perhaps eliminated. Not all countries with severe gun controls perpetrate genocide; but no genocidal governments allow any but the most politically reliable segments of the population to own guns. Because every government which in the last hundred years which has engaged in genocide has first disarmed its victim population, there is reason to believe that those governments see a relationship between gun control and the maintenance of the government's murderous power.

Today, the United Nations [UN] and gun prohibition lobbies are attempting to outlaw civilian gun ownership, especially by "non-state actors"—persons who are not approved by the government. Only the intransigence of the U.S. delegation at the July 2001 UN gun control conference prevented the creation of binding international law to forbid firearms transfer to "non-state actors"—an international law which would have prohibited the supplying of firearms to the American revolutionaries in 1776 and to the Jews in British Palestine in 1945–48, and to the resistance movements in every nation whose government formally surrendered to Hitler. The victims of contemporary genocides have the same moral right to fight for their lives as did the Jews in the Holocaust. Accordingly, Israel and other freedom-loving nations should be in the forefront of opposition to international efforts to prohibit gun ownership by groups which are targeted for genocide or are at risk of being targeted

VIEWPOINT 5

> *"If one is a follower of the Buddha, one must be a pacifist."*

Buddhism Embraces Pacifism

Ajahn Punnadhammo

Ajahn Punnadhammo is abbott of the Arrow River Forest Hermitage, a Buddhist monastery and meditation center in Northern Ontario, Canada. In the following viewpoint, he argues that Buddhism teaches that wars breed only hatred and more conflict. He says that wars are fought for gain, not for noble reasons. In conclusion, he argues that to end wars both sides must listen to each other, and the more powerful side much make the first step toward peace.

As you read, consider the following questions:

1. Punnadhammo says he receives e-mails accusing him of being unrealistic in what circumstances?
2. What does Punnadhammo say was a major cause of the Lebanon-Israel war?
3. What is Peace-It-Together, according to Punnadhammo?

My mandate . . . is to comment on current issues from a Buddhist perspective. As such, I have several times used this space to advocate against war. If one is a follower of the Buddha, one must be a pacifist. As the Buddha stated, "Hatred is never overcome by hatred, hatred is overcome by love. This is a law eternal."

Nonviolence Is Realistic

Whenever I dare to suggest that there might be better ways to resolve conflicts than air strikes and massacres, inevitably e-mails arrive accusing me of being "unrealistic." This charge is worth examining. Just how and why is it more realistic to deal with problems by violence?

Recent history certainly does not support that position. Is Iraq or the world better off because of the American invasion [of 2003]? Is Israel more secure after inflicting wholesale carnage on Lebanon [in 2006]? Has the fighting in Sri Lanka benefited either the Tamils or the Sinhalese?

The corollary of the Buddha's law is that hatred only breeds more hatred. This is particularly true in modern wars, where the technologically dominant side relies on heavy use of air power. Aerial bombardment is a nasty, and cowardly, tactic. It has the advantage of minimizing casualties among one's troops, but only at the cost of death and displacement among the hapless civilian population. And most pertinently, it creates bitterness among the survivors, breeding a new generation of terrorists.

War for Sensual Desires

In one respect the Buddhist position on war is certainly more realistic. The Buddha said that men strap on swords, and slay one another "just for sensual desires." In modern parlance, wars are fought for material gain. A study of history bears this out. The propaganda of war always claims it is for a noble goal such as democracy or civilization. Look a little closer and you find that wars are waged for land, water, oil or other resources. War is the terror of the greedy; terrorism is the war of the desperate.

The importance of oil in the Iraq war is obvious. What is less well understood is the critical role of water in the recent Lebanon-Israel war. Israel claimed to be acting to secure the release of its prisoners. But there is plenty of evidence that this campaign was planned long beforehand. Israel has a critical shortage of fresh water and there is a long history of her planners looking for ways to acquire rights to the Litani River. (For a good analysis of this Google "Israel's Water Wars" by Jason Godesky.)

It is fair to ask a pacifist, if one rejects war, how then do we solve conflicts? While there is no quick fix, a beginning must be made if we are to find peace and security or even to survive as a species. The cycle of violence and counter-violence must be broken and it usually behooves the more powerful side, as having more room to manoeuvre, to make the first step. The essential thing is a change of attitude. There must be a willingness to see the other person's humanity, and to understand the issues from their point of view. This must involve what the Zen teacher Thich Nhat Hanh calls "deep listening."

Here is a practical suggestion. Canada, as a multicultural society, has a unique opportunity to be a peacemaker. We have people living in our country from, and with connections to, all parts of the world. Why doesn't the Canadian government facilitate forums for open dialogue between representatives of warring sides; Israeli and Arab, Tamil and Sinhalese and so forth? These forums could explore ways and means to find just settlements, in a venue removed from the immediate bitterness and danger of the battlefield. A commendable private venture that does just this is Peace-It-Together which brings together Israeli and Palestinian youths to spend time together camping in the Canadian wilderness. This small first step could be greatly expanded.

Viewpoint 6

"The qualities of a good warrior are exactly the qualities needed for a serious Buddhist practitioner."

Buddhism Does Not Reject the Military

Jeanette Shin

Jeanette Shin serves in the US Navy and was commissioned as the Department of Defense's first Buddhist chaplain in 2007. In the following viewpoint, she notes that the Buddha himself first came from a warrior caste and that he often discussed spirituality in terms of military metaphors. She says that Buddhism is a religion of peace but that it accepts the reality of war. She concludes that the Buddha did not reject the military or disallow military service.

As you read, consider the following questions:

1. What is kshatriya?
2. According to Shin, the story of King Virudhaka shows that even the Buddha was unable to convince everyone to do what?
3. What does Shin say soldiers should consider before enlisting?

Jeanette Shin, "The Buddha as Warrior," wildmind.org, September 19, 2008.

The Buddha never advocated the killing or destruction of "infidels" of any religion or doctrine, and always recommended the path of nonviolence.

Buddha as Warrior

However, Shakyamuni's [the Buddha's] life and teachings reveal a person raised to be a heroic warrior invested in honor. While he renounced the life planned for him by his parents, as a secular warrior-king, he used the language of warriors to convey the Dharma [the teachings of Buddha], so he could stress that following the path of Dharma required similar virtues possessed by warriors.

Siddhartha Gautama (his birth name) was born into the kshatriya varna, or caste, of ancient India/Nepal. This was the caste of the warriors, the rulers and aristocrats of ancient India. A typical upbringing of a kshatriya male included study of the Vedas (the earliest religious texts of India) and the study of archery, swordsmanship, horsemanship, etc.

Although the Buddha's early life may sound very pampered, with his three palaces and entourage of entertainers and harem (the ancient Indian equivalent of MTV's *My [Super] Sweet Sixteen* [a reality show about wealthy teens] which would also inspire one to renounce the world), it would have been very unlikely that Siddhartha's father, King Suddhodana, would have neglected to provide this rigorous training for the presumptive heir of a small, regional power (and he did not become a world renouncer until he was about age 29).

We may see evidence of this in the language that the Buddha used in expressing Dharma: martial imagery and terms like "charioteer," "sword and shield," "war elephants," "banners," "fortress," "archers," "arrows," "poisoned arrows," are all used in expressing the struggle to overcome one's delusions and the oppositions of others.

The Buddha Was Not a Pacifist

Perhaps the most detrimental belief that has taken hold of Buddhism is pacifism; detrimental because this attitude may have contributed to the downfall of Tibet [a Buddhist nation invaded and controlled by atheist Communist China]. While the Buddha did not have to fight in physical wars, he did recognize the need to stand against evil. This is symbolized by the earth touching mudra [a symbolic gesture]. When the temptress, Mara, came to him to challenge his right to be there, he touched the ground with his right hand, signifying that he will stay in defense of the little people yet asleep to their Buddha nature. Mara and the astral forces did not want opposition to their evil designs upon an unsuspecting populace. By logic, they tried to subvert Gautama's [the Buddha's] desire to defend his right to be; his right to preserve the Path on Earth.

William House, "On Pacifism and Buddhism," Reverse Spins. www.reversespins.com.

The Battle with Evil

The Buddha's Enlightenment was described as a "battle" between himself and Mara, the embodiment of death and evil:

> King Mara, at the head of a great army of one hundred thousand, swooped down on the prince from four sides. The gods who up to that time had surrounded the prince and had sung his praises fled in fear. Now there was no one who could save the prince. But the prince thought to himself, "The Ten Precepts that I have practiced for a long period of time are my mighty army; they are the jeweled sword and the stalwart shield that guard my being. Carrying the virtuous practice of these Ten Precepts in my hand, I shall anni-

hilate the army of demons. . . . Instead of living in defeat, it is far better to do battle and die! But should they go to defeat to Mara's armies even once, mendicants and sages alike will be unable to recognize, know, or practice the path of the virtuous ones. Mara, riding atop a huge elephant, you came leading a whole army. Come, do battle! I shall emerge victorious. You will not throw me into disorder. Although the human and celestial worlds were both unable to destroy your army, I shall defeat your army as a rock destroys tree leaves."

The ancient texts emphasize the need for determination, sacrifice, and courage for Buddhists to follow the path of Buddha-dharma, to bear up under hardships in order to achieve the highest goal a human being can attain: to conquer death, fear, ignorance, evil, and thereby attain liberation. The qualities of a good warrior are exactly the qualities needed for a serious Buddhist practitioner.

As a kshatriya, the Buddha had many advantages in getting others to listen to his message, rather than if he had been born as a shudra (peasant), vaisya (merchant), or even a brahmin (priests); it is also said that the future Buddha, as a bodhisattva [enlightened one] was able to choose the time and society of his birth. The religious atmosphere of the time (5th–6th B.C.E.) witnessed a resurgence of people of this caste reexamining and questioning the authority of the brahmins, so the Buddha's teachings became popular with them, as did the teachings of his contemporary, the Jain teacher Mahavira. Other kshatriyas also likely recognized him as such (perhaps similar to the idea of "Once a Marine, always a Marine"?), possibly one reason why he was readily accepted (and protected) by the local rulers such as King Bimbisara, and which may also explain a curious story that occurs near the end of the Buddha's life.

King Virudhaka declared war against the Buddha's own clan, the Shakyas, and marched against them. The Buddha stood in his way three times. Each time King Virudhaka dismounted, paid his respects, remounted and retreated, but he kept coming back every day. By the fourth day, the Buddha did not stand in his way, and the Shakyas were defeated.

This story is very puzzling by contemporary standards: It would have been much easier for this king to simply shoot the Buddha with an arrow the first time! If he wasn't threatened, why should the Buddha not have stood there, every day, to prevent war? This story is presented as a cautionary tale on the reality of karma. At our most idealistic moments, we may like to imagine that a simple and polite expounding of the Buddha-dharma to violent and ignorant persons can end conflict, but even the Buddha himself was unable to convince everyone he met to renounce violence, or even to accept the validity of the Buddha-dharma. This teaching infers then that not even the Buddha could prevent war; war, like other acts, results from the working of karma within the realm of samsara [the world]. If the karma is present, then we may commit any sort of act, whether or not we had even planned to do it, according to Shinran Shonin [a 12th-century Japanese Buddhist monk]. As Plato said, "Only the dead do not know war." This is something to keep in mind when considering the importance of the role of the armed forces and our place within it.

Do Not Glorify War

Even given the reality of war, we should also keep in mind that the Buddha cautions against the glorification and worship of war and violence for its own sake. As is stated in the Dhammapada [a Buddhist scripture]:

> Victory breeds hatred
> The defeated live in pain,
> Happily the peaceful live,
> Giving up victory and defeat.

There is no Buddhist version of 'Valhalla.' Everyone is responsible for his or her own karma, and should be mindful of what our present and future actions may entail, which is the causing of death and death for ourselves in battle. Preferably, people should consider this before enlisting! Even though we have voluntarily accepted this path, we should also be prepared to accept the karmic results, and also know that, like any career, our own military path will end one way or another.

The military life is not for everyone. As servicemembers, especially those in leadership positions and those who have been in for awhile, we know that some are simply not cut out for military service, whether it is because, on one end, they are whiners, "dirtbags" (I'm sure many people in the military have heard this word before) and outright criminals, or others who, although not bad people, simply can't adjust to the military lifestyle.

I'm sure many of us have encountered these individuals, and also knew that the best thing for all concerned was for them to get out and go home (preferably as quickly as possible). But we've also known others who become very successful, who take to the military life and deployments like fish to water, look out for their people, and thrive on the warrior lifestyle, hardships and all. Chaplains see this all the time. Therefore, there are many different teachings in the Buddhist canon concerning the use of force and conflict, just as counseling is different for different individuals, just as not all wars are alike.

The Buddha must have encountered many similar situations in talking to people from different castes and professions, some he may never have associated with before, like barbers and shopkeepers; we also know that he included kings and their warriors in his audiences. We do know that he admitted them to his presence, and talked to them, advising some to renounce the life of a warrior, others he would not admit in the Sangha [the Buddhist community], until after they had completed their military service. He did not shun them because of their profession. He had been one of them.

Periodical and Internet Sources Bibliography

The following articles have been selected to supplement the diverse views presented in this chapter.

Michael Broyde	"Pacifism in Jewish Law," My Jewish Learning. www.myjewishlearning.com.
Phil Elmore	"Why the Buddhist Peace Fellowship Is Wrong," *Martialist*, December 14, 2009.
Great Hindu	"The Hindu Concept of War," February 26, 2008. http://greathindu.com.
Usama Hassan	"Recapturing Islam from the Pacifists," Islamic Awakening, November 14, 2001. www.islamicawakening.com.
William House	"On Pacifism and Buddhism," Reverse Spins. www.reversespins.com.
Learn Peace	"World Religions: War and Peace." www.ppu.org.uk.
Muhammad Legenhausen	"Islamic Just War Pacifism," AhlulBayt Islamic Mission, March 12, 2008. http://www.aimislam.com.
Sumanto al Qurtuby	"Strengthening the Pacifist Islam," *Jaringan Islam Liberal*, July 16, 2008.
Aaron J. Tapper	"Hamas Pacifists and Settler Islamophiles," *Tikkun*, July–August 2005.
Arthur O. Waskow	"Assertive Nonviolence in Judaism," My Jewish Learning. www.myjewishlearning.com.

OPPOSING VIEWPOINTS® SERIES

CHAPTER 3

What Are Secular Pacifist Traditions?

Chapter Preface

Many pacifists are inspired by religious faith. However, there is also a secular tradition of pacifism. One of the most well-known secular practitioners of nonviolence was the historian and writer Howard Zinn, best known for his book *A People's History of the United States.*

Zinn fought in the US Army Air Forces during World War II, where he bombed targets in Berlin, Czechoslovakia, and Hungary. He was also involved in the first military use of napalm, an extremely flammable substance that causes severe burns and explosions. In a 2004 interview with Joel Whitney of *Guernica*, Zinn noted that while he was a bomber he had not seen his actions as wrong. However, after reading about the aftermath of Hiroshima, Zinn realized the horrors he had inflicted. He concluded, "I began to think of war—even a war with as moral a purpose as World War II (that is, getting rid of [Nazi leader Adolf] Hitler)—as being inadequate, really, to solve fundamental problems. I began to think of war, even so-called 'good wars' like World War II, as corrupting everybody. Violence begetting violence."

Zinn became a well-known writer and activist on behalf of social justice. His antiwar stance was an important part of his political commitment. He was an outspoken critic of the Vietnam War, writing books against the conflict including *Vietnam: The Logic of Withdrawal* (1967) and *Disobedience and Democracy: Nine Fallacies on Law and Order* (1968). He risked prosecution by helping to get the Pentagon Papers, a collection of secret government documents that revealed the Lyndon B. Johnson administration had lied about the war, to the *New York Times.*

After Vietnam, Zinn continued to strongly oppose war and violence. In a December 2001 issue of the *Progressive*, for example, he spoke out against the US invasion of Afghanistan, arguing that "the September 11 [2001] attack [by terrorists on the World Trade Center and Pentagon] constitutes a crime against humanity and cannot be justified, and the bombing of Afghanistan is also a crime, which cannot be justified."

In that same article, Zinn explained that he did not see himself as an absolute pacifist, because circumstances might in some cases require "a small, focused act of violence" against evil. However, he argued that wars could never be justified in this way and that the killing of millions of innocent people was always evil. "Pacifism," he said, "which I define as a rejection of war, rests on a very powerful logic. In war, the means—indiscriminate killing—are immediate and certain; the ends, however desirable, are distant and uncertain."

Zinn's pacifism, then, rested not on religious doctrine or belief, but on personal experience and on an evaluation of the practical costs of war. The following viewpoints discuss other secular arguments for and against nonviolence.

VIEWPOINT 1

> *"In the real world . . . pacifism is a sound guide to action."*

Pacifism Is a Commonsense Philosophy

Bryan Caplan

Bryan Caplan is associate professor of economics at George Mason University and an adjunct scholar for the Cato Institute. In the following viewpoint, he argues that pacifism should be seen as an opposition to war, rather than as an opposition to all violence. He says to be morally justified the benefits of war must substantially outweigh the short-run costs. This situation, he argues, hardly ever occurs, since the costs of war are very high and the benefits are uncertain.

As you read, consider the following questions:

1. Why does Caplan argue that it is virtually impossible to fight a war of self-defense?
2. What does Caplan believe the innocent lives saved/innocent lives lost ratio would have to be to justify a war?

3. Caplan says that pacifism is the radical notion that what?

I used to call myself an isolationist, but I recently realized that *pacifist* is a much better description of my position. All of the following definitions aptly describe what I believe:

Defining Pacifism

- pacifism: The doctrine that disputes (especially between countries) should be settled without recourse to violence; the active opposition to such violence, especially the refusal to take part in military action
- pacifist: opposed to war
- pacifist: one who loves, supports, or favors peace; one who is pro-peace
- pacifist: an individual who disagrees with war on principle

Some definitions of pacifism specify opposition to all violence, even in self-defense, but these strike me as too broad. I'm a pacifist not because I *oppose* self-defense, but because it's virtually impossible to fight a war of self-defense. Even if militaries don't deliberately target innocent bystanders, they almost always wind up recklessly endangering their lives. If a policeman fought crime the way that "civilized" armies wage war, we'd put him in jail.

But isn't pacifism, in [cartoon character] Homer Simpson's words, one of those views "with all the well-meaning rules that don't work in real life"? No. Here's my commonsense case for pacifism:

1. The immediate costs of war are clearly awful. Most wars lead to massive loss of life and wealth on at least one side. If you use a standard value of life of $5M [million], every 200,000 deaths is equivalent to a *trillion* dollars of damage.

2. The long-run benefits of war are highly uncertain. Some wars—most obviously the Napoleonic Wars [in Europe from 1803 to 1815] and World War II—at least arguably deserve credit for decades of subsequent peace. But many other wars—like the French Revolution and World War I—just sowed the seeds for new and greater horrors. You could say, "Fine, let's only fight wars with big long-run benefits." In practice, however, it's very difficult to predict a war's long-run consequences. One of the great lessons of [Philip E.] Tetlock's *Expert Political Judgment*[1] is that foreign policy experts are *much* more certain of their predictions than they have any right to be.

3. For a war to be morally justified, its long-run benefits have to be substantially larger than its short-run costs. I call this "the principle of mild deontology." Almost everyone thinks it's wrong to murder a random person and use his organs to save the lives of five other people. For a war to be morally justified, then, its (innocent lives saved/innocent lives lost) ratio would have to exceed 5:1. (I personally think that a much higher ratio is morally required, but I don't need that assumption to make my case).

Are there conceivable circumstances under which I'd break my pacifist principles? Yes; as I explained in my debate with [economist] Robin Hanson [on Liberty vs. Efficiency, held on April 14, 2009], I oppose "one-sentence moral theories":

> It is absurd to latch on to an abstract grand moral theory, and then defend it against every counterexample.

A Sound Guide

In the real world, however, pacifism is a sound guide to action. While I admit that wars occasionally have good overall consequences, it's very difficult to identify these wars in ad-

1. *Expert Political Judgment* is a 2005 book that followed the predictions of 284 political experts over twenty years. The study found the forecasters did only slightly better than chance.

vance. And unless you're willing to bite the bullet of involuntary organ donation, "good overall consequences" are insufficient to morally justify war. If the advocates of a war can't reasonably claim that they're saving five times as many innocent lives as they take, they're in the wrong.

I suspect that economists' main objection to pacifism is it actually *increases* the quantity of war by reducing the cost of aggressions [that is, if you are not going to be opposed to violence, you are more likely to act aggressively]. As I've argued before, though, this is at best a half-truth:

> Threats and bullying don't just *move along* the "demand for crossing you" curve.[2] If your targets perceive your behavior as inappropriate, mean, or downright evil, it *shifts* their "demand for crossing you" out [or, in other words, the demand for crossing you increases]. Call it psychology, or just common sense: People who previously bore you no ill will now start looking for a chance to give you a taste of your own medicine.
>
> The upshot for foreign policy is that people who warn about "sowing the seeds of hate" are not the simpletons they often seem to be. Military reprisals against, for example, nations that harbor terrorists reduce the quantity of terrorism holding anti-U.S. hatred fixed. But if people in target countries and those who sympathize with them feel the reprisals are unjustified, we are making them angrier and thereby increasing the demand for terrorism. Net effect: *Ambiguous.*

Rebecca West [a journalist and author] once wrote that, "Feminism is the radical notion that women are people." Pacifism, similarly, is the radical notion that before you kill innocent people, you should be reasonably sure that your action will have very good consequences. That's a one-sentence moral theory even I'm comfortable embracing.

2. In economics, a demand curve is a graph showing what price consumers will pay for a good.

Viewpoint 2

"The problem with atheist pacifism is that . . . one is sacrificing one's only chance to fend off terrible evil."

Secular Pacifism Does Not Make Sense

Robert M. Price

Robert M. Price is professor of theology and scriptural studies at Johnnie Colemon Theological Seminary and the founder and editor of the Journal of Higher Criticism. *In the following viewpoint, he argues that pacifism is logically based on the idea that you should suffer violence on earth in order to earn peace in heaven. Price claims, therefore, that atheist pacifism is logically inconsistent, since there is no afterlife to justify the refusal to fight for justice in this world. Price also says pacifism is based on cowardice and that it would allow evil men like Adolf Hitler to perpetrate atrocities unchecked.*

As you read, consider the following questions:

1. What Christian ideas does Price suggest can lead to a philosophy of anarchism?
2. According to Price, total pacifism is the heritage of what?

Robert M. Price, "Sheep in Wolves' Clothing," Robertmprice.com, 2005.

3. What argument for pacifism does Price say caused him to reject pacifism?

It is no mystery why wolves might disguise themselves as sheep, if they thought of it. In that way they might entice sheep into their hungry care. We are told sheep are pretty stupid, so they might well fall for it. It is baffling, however, to contemplate why sheep might masquerade as wolves. Suppose one did, and a real wolf began to catch on. Suppose he penetrated the disguise. He might well go on to eat the hapless sheep. But first one can imagine him questioning the sheep on his suicidal strategy. What could the wolf-clad sheep hope to gain by such a pretense? Espionage? Not likely; the ways of wolves are too well known already. Was there perhaps some sort of envy? Had the sheep come to tire of the dull ways of his woolly clan? Did the roguish life of the wolves attract him? Who can guess? It hardly matters. Sheep never do this. But people do.

Some Atheists Embrace Christian Ethics

Why do professed atheists today, in great numbers, seem to embrace social ethics that mirror in startling ways the stance of Christianity, and even of an extreme form of radical Christianity? I am thinking of the noble-seeming opposition of humanists and atheists to capital punishment, as well as their espousal of pacifism. We must ask how well such beliefs fit into the very different frameworks of atheism and Christianity.

Opposition to capital punishment seems to be based on the theological belief that all lives are automatically *ipso facto* sacred, and that human beings never have the right to deprive even the foulest criminal of his or her life. On the one hand, there is the belief that all human lives are created in the image of God and thus possess ineradicable human dignity, which is then extended to imply an inviolable right to life. On the other hand, there is an implicitly anarchistic assumption, reflected in the apocryphal tale of Jesus and the woman taken in adultery: "Let him who is without sin cast the first stone." Only God has the privileged position to presume to judge humans, we are told here. That is the recipe for anarchism [a belief that there should be no government], and there have been Christian anarchists.

As I understand it, atheists base their belief in human rights on a Social Compact model. Having no creator, it is up to us to decide what are human rights and responsibilities based on what arrangement will maximize social and individual freedoms. Certain things will work to safeguard a harmonious society, others will not. It is a great game, and one retains rights as long as one observes commensurate responsibilities. Sometimes, as in war, the maintenance of social order necessitates the taking of life (or does it? Yes, but see below). The murderer (and perhaps other criminals, too) has forfeited his own rights by denying those of others. He has lost the right to life. He is ejected from the game.

As for any mere human having the right to judge, we have over time developed a rational (though admittedly fallible) system that makes administration of justice far more impartial by removing it from the control of interested parties. To escape the dangerous situation of vendetta justice, which degenerates quickly into epidemic violence, justice first passed into the system of scapegoat justice, where blame was transferred to a surrogate victim, eventually an animal. After that, justice was assigned by impartial judges with no relation to anyone in the case. The judge need not be without sin, just without bribe. Atheists certainly do not think justice is impossible because it will likely never be perfect. We have to do the best we can with what (and who) we've got, namely us.

Moral Decadence

It seems to me that the liberal and radical opposition to capital punishment is a blatant case of the moral decadence [19th-century philosopher Friedrich] Nietzsche blamed on Christianity. Why? The spectacle of bleeding-heart protesters holding a candlelight vigil for the latest convicted serial killer shows this perversity in the starkest possible light. Such protesters imagine that there is no moral difference between the unfeeling murderer and the state who executes him, as if "killing" were the only relevant feature defining the situation. That is absurd, like placing [German dictator Adolf] Hitler and his victims on the same level. Don't you see where this irony comes from? For one thing, it stems directly from the herd mentality whereby the cringing slave seeks refuge in a mass of morally equal faceless drones. Let no one be judged on merit! The doctrine of salvation by grace, whereby all are deemed equal in God's sight, is, as [19th-century German philosopher Ludwig Andreas von] Feuerbach knew, the refuge of the guilty coward. See? If [serial killer] Jeffrey Dahmer can't be held responsible, then neither can I, for I will never be guilty of anything remotely so bad!

It is a moral version of the reluctance of teachers' unions to accept professional competency testing or merit pay. How much safer to take refuge in the miasma of the collective which no one ever calls to task. Objectors to capital punishment are reducing the killer and the state to what [French historian] René Girard calls "mimetic doubles," between whom no moral distinction can any more be drawn. And this is to upend the rules of the only game in town, the Social Compact. Why should atheists join the religious in crusading on behalf of their dogma that all human lives are to be protected no matter what?

Pacifism Is Logically Christian

Now, to war. Not all or even most Christians oppose it. Strictly, total pacifism is the heritage of the Radical Reformation[1]

1. The Radical Reformation was a 16th-century Protestant movement that rejected elite church authority.

Pacifism Is Impractical

While I understand and share the respect for human life that underlies the pacifist philosophy . . . I cannot join in the naive and dangerous belief that a person should allow a violent criminal to kill them or another innocent person. . . .

I don't wish to see innocent people suffer and die at the hands of a criminal—and a gun is the best way yet invented by humankind to stop a violent criminal.

Eric D. Puryear,
"Pacifism—A Naive and Dangerous Approach to Life,"
LearnAboutGuns.com, October 3, 2008.
www.learnaboutguns.com.

(Amish, Mennonites, Church of the Brethren, Dunkers) and groups following in their footsteps (some Baptists, Quakers). What is the thinking here? They believe that Jesus forbade warfare when he urged people not to respond in kind when slapped or abused. Whether one can extrapolate from this to national defense is a complex hermeneutical question, but that is the extrapolation pacifists make. It is important to see how pacifism is rooted not just historically but logically in the ethic of Christianity. The very idea presupposes the Christian hope of salvation. The radical Christian will gladly suffer martyrdom for his refusal to shed his enemy's blood, if it comes to that (and it would very quickly once a hypothetical nation of pacifists were invaded by Nazis). In this he is proud to follow in the footsteps of his Jewish predecessors who were willing to die under torture rather than eat the forbidden pork. Why did courageous Jews and Christians consider these trades fair ones? Because they believed it would gain them the martyr's crown in heaven. If one does not harbor such an expectation, the trade may not seem so reasonable.

Of course, many atheists are patriots and would gladly give their lives for their country and its way of life. Sometimes one can do no other. The rule is not to save one's skin at any cost. But the problem with atheist pacifism is that by beating one's sword into a harmless ploughshare, one is sacrificing one's only chance to fend off terrible evil. There will be no better heaven than this. We had better do what is needful to secure it, for our children if not for ourselves. And this means the willingness both to give and to take life.

I once believed in pacifism—until I heard an eloquent defense of it. We were at Princeton Theological Seminary. I was talking to a man who had given up ministerial training to take up the law. He wanted to serve the urban poor who could not afford high-priced lawyers. A radical Christian, to be sure, and, sure enough, a pacifist. Someone asked the inevitable question: If he was so opposed to using force to repel aggression, what would he do should he discover some intruder making ready to rape his wife? His answer? He would not use violence because that would show a lack of faith both in his wife's ingenuity to extricate herself from the situation, and in God who might be planning some miraculous deliverance at the last possible moment. I had heard enough.

Fear Masquerading as Compassion

But I hadn't heard it all. Not by a long shot. Because now I have heard of pacifist atheists. I must conclude that they have caught the Christian disease of undiscriminating moral decadence: They equate the victim and the victimizer, and they are just plain soft on crooks because they lack the guts to do anything about it. Fear masquerades as compassion.

Sometimes one hears atheists absolutely ruling out war because of the supposed rationalism on which they like to congratulate themselves. War is always a failure of diplomacy.

True enough. But sometimes, as Neville Chamberlain[2] discovered, diplomacy is a game one cannot win. Someone is cheating. Someone is taking advantage of the professed refusal of one side ever to resort to force. They are playing the pacifists for the fools they are, to get as far as they can before they have to start shooting, knowing we may well be intimidated into giving up the store before they have to rob it! This, too, is Christian decadence in disguise. It shows a stance of pure and unsupported faith which facts cannot penetrate until it is much too late. The liberal atheist, like his fideistic Christian model, simply refuses to accept certain harsh realities. As [psychoanalyst Sigmund] Freud said of the religious believer, the invulnerable liberal is remaking the real world into a wish world by projecting his own values upon it. And the real world is one that contains aggressive people who want to take what you have and do not believe, as liberals do, that there are always two sides to every dispute. You can be sure that fanatics like Osama bin Laden [leader of the terrorist organization al Qaeda] do not think for a second that there is a rational "solution" to a "problem" that would avert war any more than Hitler did. Look at facts, empiricist! Nietzsche said, "Faith is not wanting to know the truth." Does your politics allow you to know it?

2. Neville Chamberlain was British prime minister at the time of Hitler's rise to power. Chamberlain agreed to allow Hitler to annex land in exchange for peace. Hitler went on to violate the agreement, and Chamberlain's negotiations have since been much criticized.

Viewpoint 3

> *"Instead of fantasizing about pending calamities that might happen, think about the calamities that are happening now: war, poverty, and the degradations of violence sanctioned by political power and laws."*

Pacifism Based on Anarchism Is a Workable Model for Peace

Colman McCarthy

Colman McCarthy is a writer, teacher, former Washington Post *columnist, and the founder and director of the Center for Teaching Peace. In the following viewpoint, he argues that anarchy is not chaos. Instead, he says that chaos is caused by states that commit violence and launch wars. He suggests that anarchists should embrace pacifism as an alternative to state violence and notes that many revolutions have been accomplished by nonviolent means. He concludes by suggesting that individuals should make personal commitments to anarchist nonviolence by refusing to support immoral companies and through lifestyle choices such as vegetarianism and bicycling.*

Colman McCarthy, "Anarchism, Education, and the Road to Peace," *Contemporary Anarchist Studies: An Introductory Anthology of Anarchy in the Academy*. New York: Routledge, 2009. pp. 175–80. Reproduced by permission.

As you read, consider the following questions:

1. What action was taken by Congress following Kropotkin's second lecture tour?
2. According to McCarthy, what places has the United States bombed in the last sixty years?
3. Name a few recent examples that McCarthy provides of situations in which nonviolent conflict resolution has worked.

One of the major draws on the US lecture circuit some one hundred years ago was Prince Peter Kropotkin. In October 1897, the revered "father" of modern anarchism, who was born to nobility in Moscow in 1842, addressed the National Geographic Society in Washington [D.C.]. In New York City he lectured to audiences of 2,000 people. In Boston, large crowds at Harvard and other sites heard him speak on the ideas found in his classic works, *Mutual Aid; Fields, Factories and Workshops*; . . . and *The Conquest of Bread*. Admission was 15 cents, sometimes a quarter, or else free so that (as Kropotkin desired) "ordinary workers" would be able to attend. Kropotkin came back to America for another tour in 1901. In Chicago, Jane Addams, the director of Hull House who would win the Nobel Peace Prize in 1931, was his host. Emma Goldman (who believed that "organized violence" from the "top" creates "individual violence" at the "bottom") and [lawyer] Clarence Darrow praised him then, as would [historian and philosopher] Lewis Mumford, [anthropologist] Ashley Montagu, and [journalist] I.F. Stone years later.

A Popular Message of Peace

The prince, a serene and kindly activist-philosopher and the antithesis of the will-eyed bomb throwers who commonly come to mind when anarchism is mentioned in polite or impolite company, enjoyed packed houses when the military muscles of American interventionism were being flexed with great fervor. In 1896, Marines were dispatched to Corinto, Nicaragua, under the guise of protecting US lives and property during a revolt. In 1898, Marines were stationed at Tientsin and Peking, China, to ensure the safety of Americans caught in the conflict between the dowager empress and her son. The following year, Marines were sent to Bluefields, Nicaragua, to keep their version of the peace. Then it was back to China, ordered there by the [President William] McKinley administration to protect American interests during the Boxer Rebellion [an anticolonialist, anti-Christian movement].

Political Washington couldn't fail to notice that Kropotkin was on the loose, going from one podium to another denouncing the favored form of governmental coercion, the military:

> Wars for the possession of the East, wars for the empire of the sea, wars to impose duties on imports and to dictate conditions to neighboring states, wars against those "blacks" who revolt! The roar of the cannon never ceases in the world, whole races are massacred, the states of Europe spend a third of their budget on armaments; and we know how heavily these taxes fall on the workers.

Unfortunately, we don't know, or choose not to know. If it were the opposite, the lives and thoughts of nineteenth- and twentieth-century anarchists would be as discussed and studied in schools as those of the politicians who raise the funds for wars and the militarists who are paid to do the killing. After Kropotkin's second lecture tour, with the crowds growing larger and the prince's message growing bolder, Congress took action. It passed a law in 1903 forbidding anarchists to enter the country. In a letter to Emma Goldman, Kropotkin described an addled and anxious America that "throws its hypocritical liberties overboard, tears them to pieces—as soon as people use those liberties for fighting that cursed society."

In the courses on pacifism and nonviolence that I've been teaching in law school, university, and high school classes since 1982, students get full exposure to Kropotkin. In the first minutes of the semester, I cite the Russian's counsel to students: "Think about the kind of world you want to live and work in. What do you need to build that world? Demand that your teachers teach you that." Hidebound as they are to take required three-credit courses that current curricula impose on students, and a bit unsteady on exactly how to pursue the art of demanding, only a few are up to acting on Kropotkin's call. For me, it's a victory if students make demands on themselves and dive into Kropotkin on their own, inching a bit closer to a theoretical understanding of anarchy.

Anarchy Is Not Chaos

To get their minds in motion, I ask students what word they first think of when anarchy is mentioned. "Chaos," they answer, "anarchy is chaos." I am consistently surprised by their responses linking anarchy with chaos. However, when I conceptualize chaos, these types of questions come to mind: What about the 40-odd wars or conflicts currently [in 2009] raging on the world's known and unknown battlefields? Isn't it chaotic that between 35,000 and 40,000 people die every day of hunger or preventable diseases? Doesn't economic chaos prevail when large numbers of the world's poor earn less than $1 dollar a day? Isn't environmental chaos looming as the climate warms? Aren't America's prisons, which house mentally ill or drug-addicted inmates who need to be treated more than stashed, scenes of chaos? All of these questions address the real chaos that is occurring in the world today. Anarchists aren't causing all that, but rather (it might be said) are trying to prevent it. Instead, it falls on those lawmaking legislatures instructing the citizens, raised to be faithful law-abiders, on what is the public good: Laws. Laws. Laws. They make us more "civilized," say our lawmaking betters. The problem is, laws are made by people and people are often wrong, so why place your faith in wrongheadedness?

The root word of anarchy is *arch*, Greek for rule. A half dozen archs are in play. Monarchy: the royals rule. Patriarchy: the fathers rule. Oligarchy: the rich few rule. Gynarchy: women rule. Stretching it a bit, there is Noah's-archy: the animals rule. (Pardon the pun. No, wait. Don't pardon it. A certain strain of anarchists, I fear, tends to brood, so a laugh now and again can be useful.) And then we arrive at anarchy, where no one rules. Fright and fear creep into students' minds, especially those who suspect that anarchists are high-energy people with chronic wild streaks. With no rules, no laws, and no governments, what will happen? The question is speculative, but instead of fantasizing about pending calamities that might happen, think about the calamities that are happening now: war, poverty, and the degradations of violence sanctioned by political power and laws. Indeed, as Kropotkin himself once warned:

> We are so perverted by an education which from infancy seeks to kill in us the spirit of revolt, and to develop that of submission to authority; we are so perverted by this existence under the ferrule of a law, which regulates every event in life—our birth, our education, our development, our love, our friendship—that, if this state of things continues, we shall lose all initiative, all habit of thinking for ourselves. Our society seems no longer able to understand that it is possible to exist otherwise than under the reign of law, elaborated by a representative government and administered by a handful of rulers. And even when it has gone so far as to emancipate itself from the thralldom, its first care has been to reconstitute it immediately.

Extending these points, on November 17, 1921, [Indian revolutionary] Mohandas [Mahatma] Gandhi wrote in his journal:

> Political power means the capacity to regulate national life through national representatives. If national life becomes so perfect as to become self-regulated, no representation becomes necessary. There is then a state of enlightened anarchy. In such a state everyone is his own ruler. He rules himself in such a manner that he is never a hindrance to his neighbor. In the ideal state, therefore, there is no political power because there is no state.

Do Not Legislate; Educate

The solution to the dilemma, at least in the anarchism to which I subscribe, is to remember that either we legislate to fear or educate to goodness. Law-abiding citizens are fear-abiding citizens, who fear being caught when a law is broken or disobeyed. Fined. Shamed. Punished. When a child is educated to goodness, beginning in a family where the adults have a talent or two in solving their conflicts without physical or emotional violence, he or she is exposed to lessons of kindness, cooperation, and empathy that leads to what might be called "the good life."

Anarchists, especially when they dress in all black and mass-migrate to protests at the World Bank or International Monetary Fund conclaves, don't do much to persuade the public to sign on when they shout epithets at the hapless bureaucrats and papercrats crawling into work. The verbal violence serves mostly to reinforce the perception that anarchists are more generally violent, conjuring the age-old image of the bomb-thrower. It's true enough that anarchists have thrown bombs in isolated demonstrations, although we know that the greater threat are the bomb-droppers (beginning with the two atomic bombs dropped on the Japanese people, and the 35 more tested in the Marshall Islands during the late 1940s and early 1950s—not to mention US bombings in the last 60 years of China, Korea, Guatemala, Indonesia, Cuba, Congo, Peru, Laos, Vietnam, Cambodia, Grenada, Libya, El Salvador, Nicaragua, Panama, Iraq, Afghanistan, Yugoslavia, and Yemen, to name a few, constituting what Martin Luther King Jr. once called "the world's greatest purveyor of violence"). To me, and to counter the violence of the state, anarchism needs to be twinned with pacifism. Violent anarchism is self-defeating, and bangs its head into the truth once stated by [political theorist] Hannah Arendt in her essential work *On Violence*: "Violence, like all action, changes the world, but the most probable change is to a more violent world."

And yet, if any creed is less understood than anarchism, it is pacifism. The uneducated equate it with passivity. The really uneducated pair it with appeasement. Among the latter is the late Michael Kelly, whose column "Pacifist Claptrap" ran on the *Washington Post* op-ed page on September 26, 2001:

> Organized terrorist groups have attacked Americans [in the September 11, 2001, attacks]. These groups wish the Americans not to fight. The American pacifists wish the Americans not to fight. If the Americans do not fight, the terrorists will attack America again. . . . The American pacifists, therefore, are on the side of future mass murders of Americans. They are objectively pro-terrorist.

A week later he was back with more, in a column arguing that pacifists are liars, frauds, and hypocrites whose position is "evil." Kelly, whose shrillness matched his self-importance, was regrettably killed in Iraq in April 2003, reporting on a US invasion that he avidly and slavishly promoted.

Pacifism Works

The pacifist position on countering terrorism was more astutely articulated by Archbishop Desmond Tutu in a lecture on February 24, 2002, at St. Paul's Cathedral in Boston: "The war against terrorism will not be won as long as there are people desperate with disease and living in poverty and squalor. Sharing our prosperity is the best weapon against terrorism." Instead of sharing its wealth, however, the United States government hoards it. Among the top 25 industrial nations, it ranks 24th in the percentage of its GNP [gross national product] devoted to foreign aid.

Furthermore, pacifists are routinely told that nonviolent conflict resolution is a noble theory, but asked where has it worked. Had questioners paid only slight attention these past years, the answer would be obvious: in plenty of places, as the following list of recent examples nicely illustrates.

- On February 26, 1986, a frightened Ferdinand Marcos, once a ruthless dictator and a US-supported thug hailed by [former president] Jimmy Carter as a champion of human rights, fled from the Philippines to exile in Hawaii. As staged by nuns, students, and workers who were trained by Gene Sharp of the [Albert] Einstein [Institution] in Boston, a three-year nonviolent revolt brought Marcos down.
- On October 5, 1988, Chile's despot and another US favorite, General Augusto Pinochet, was driven from office after five years of strikes, boycotts and other forms of nonviolent resistance. A Chilean organizer who led the demand for free elections said: "We didn't protest with arms. That gave us more power."
- On August 24, 1989, in Poland, the Soviet Union puppet regime of General Wojciech Jaruzelski fell. On that day it peacefully ceded power to a coalition government created by the Solidarity labor union that, for a decade, used nonviolent strategies to overthrow the Communist dictator. Few resisters were killed in the nine-year struggle. The example of Poland's nonviolence spread, with the Soviet Union's collapse soon coming. It was the daring deeds of Lech Walesa, Nobel Peace Prize winner, and the nonviolent Poles on the barricades with him that were instrumental in bringing about this change.

- On May 10, 1994, former political prisoner Nelson Mandela became the president of South Africa. It was not armed combat that ended white supremacy. It was the moral force of organized nonviolent resistance that made it impossible for the racist government to control the justice-demanding population.
- On April 1, 2001, in Yugoslavia, Serbian police arrested Slobodan Milosevic for his crimes while in office. In the two years that a student-led protest rallied citizens to defy the dictator, not one resister was killed by the government. The tyrant died during his trial in The Hague.
- On November 23, 2003, the bloodless "revolution of the roses" toppled Georgian president Eduard Shevardnadze. Unlike the civil war that marked the power struggles in the 1990s, no deaths or injuries occurred when tens of thousands of Georgians took to the streets of Tblisi in the final surge to oust the government.

Weapons of the Spirit

Twenty-five years ago who would have thought that any of these examples would be possible? Yet they happened. Ruthless regimes, backed by torture chambers and death squads, were driven from power by citizens who had no guns, tanks, bombs, or armies. They had an arsenal far superior to weapons of steel: weapons of the spirit. These were on display in the early 1940s when [German dictator Adolf] Hitler's Nazi army invaded Denmark. Led by a defiant King Christian X, the Danes organized strikes, boycotts, and work stoppages, and either hid Jews in their homes or helped them flee to Sweden or Norway. Of this resistance, an historian quoted in the landmark 2000 film *A Force More Powerful* observed that

> Denmark had not won the war but neither had it been defeated or destroyed. Most Danes had not been brutalized, by the Germans or each other. Nonviolent resistance saved the country and contributed more to the Allied victory Danish arms ever could have done.

Only one member of Congress voted no against US entry into the Second World War: Jeannette Rankin, a pacifist from Montana who came to the House of Representatives in 1916, four years before the 19th amendment gave women the vote. "You can no more win a war than win an earthquake," she famously said before casting her vote. The public reaction reached so strong a virulence that Rankin had to be given 24-hour police protection. One of her few allies that year was Helen Keller, the deaf and sightless Socialist who spoke in Carnegie Hall in New York:

> Strike against war, for without you no battles can be fought. Strike against manufacturing shrapnel and gas bombs and all other tools of murder. Strike against preparedness that means death and misery to millions of human beings. Be not dumb obedient slaves in an army of destruction. Be heroes in an army of construction.

Personalize the Struggle

Students leaning toward anarchism and pacifism often ask how the principles of both can be personalized. I suggest that one start by examining where you spend your money. Deny it to any company that despoils the earth. Deny it to any seller of death, whether Lockheed Martin (the country's largest weapons maker) or to subcontractors scattered in small towns in all regions of the land. Deny it to the establishment media that asks few meaningful questions and questions few meaningless answers. In short, "live simply so others may simply live," which is perhaps the purest form of anarchy.

In my own life, I've tried to do it by means of a cruelty-free vegan diet, consuming no alcohol, caffeine, or nicotine, and getting around Washington mostly by a trusty Raleigh three-speed bicycle. Is any machine more philosophically suited to anarchism than a bicycle? Is there an easier way to practice anarchism than joyriding on two wheels? Being street-smart, which means being totally considerate of other travelers and pedaling safely, I think of all the useless laws the anarchist-cyclist can break: riding through red lights, stop signs, one-way signs—all the while getting a feel for outdoor life and its weathers, those balms cut off by windshields.

Speaking experientially—meaning 35 years and more than 70,000 miles of motion by leg power—I've become an autophobe. In the clog of traffic, when car owners are penned like cattle on a factory farm and torture themselves in massive tie-ups, I remember some lines by Daniel Behrman in his minor 1973 classic from *Harper's* magazine, "The Man Who Loved Bicycles":

> The bicycle is a vehicle for revolution. It can destroy the tyranny of the automobile as effectively as the printing press brought down despots of flesh and blood. The revolution will be spontaneous, the sum total of individual revolts like my own. It may already have begun.

William Saroyan likewise wrote in his introduction to 1981's edited volume *The Noiseless Tenor* that "the bicycle is the noblest invention of [hu]mankind." Amen to that, but only if you add that anarchism is a close second.

Viewpoint 4

> *"The vision of anarcho-pacifists is noble and something we should aspire to—when civilization is finally ready to accommodate it."*

Pacifism Based on Anarchism Is Not Workable

Ladd Everitt

Ladd Everitt is director of communications at the Coalition to Stop Gun Violence. In the following viewpoint, he argues that anarchism, or the elimination of government, will not lead to nonviolence. Instead, he argues, in America the abolition of laws would result in a wave of violence by right-wing nationalist, racist groups. He concludes that anarchist pacifism is an ideal that may be possible at some point in the future but that it is not a practical possibility at the moment.

As you read, consider the following questions:

1. What is Colman McCarthy's response to those who fantasize about pending calamities in a world without government?
2. According to Everitt, what is *The Turner Diaries?*

3. What did Martin Luther King Jr. say could not be legislated, and what did he say could be regulated, according to Everitt?

One idea that I find intriguing is the notion that peace can be obtained through anarchy, which *Webster's* defines as "a utopian society of individuals who enjoy complete freedom without government." One of the original proponents of this concept was [19th-century Russian author] Leo Tolstoy. Tolstoy believed that *all* violence was wrong, including personal self-defense against imminent attack. Furthermore, as [Russian Prince] Peter Kropotkin wrote: "Robbers, [Tolstoy] says, are far less dangerous than a well-organized government."

Anarchy Leads to Violence

These convictions continue to inspire pacifists today. Colman McCarthy, the director of American University's Center for Teaching Peace, bemoans the fact that, in the minds of his students, the word "anarchy" invariably means "chaos." His reply? "Instead of fantasizing about the pending calamites that might happen, think about the calamities that are happening now: war, poverty, and the degradations of violence sanctioned by political power and laws."

McCarthy worries that youth that "dress in all black and mass-migrate to protests at the World Bank" have given anarchists a bad name by engaging in "verbal violence." But these are not the people I would worry about if the government was disbanded.

Instead, my mind turns to the immediate aftermath of Hurricane Katrina [a 2005 hurricane that devastated New Orleans], when a heavily armed private militia patrolled the streets of predominantly white Algiers Point and shot African Americans at will.

I think about [conservative commentator] Glenn Beck's 2014 civil war scenario called "The Bubba Effect," where angry

The Turner Diaries and Far-Right Extremism

The Turner Diaries is probably the most widely read book among Far-Right extremists; many have cited it as the inspiration behind their terrorist . . . activity. Hoping to bring about the Aryan uprising depicted in [the] novel, Robert Mathews . . . helped found the 1980s' white supremacist gang The Order. Mathews's efforts ended in a fatal shootout with FBI agents in 1984, while other Order members . . . were . . . sentenced to long prison terms for their crimes, . . . which included murders, robberies, . . . and the bombing of a synagogue.

Anti-Defamation League, "The Turner Diaries: Extremism in America," 2005. www.adl.org.

Americans hole up in armed camps in the South and West and shoot anyone who comes near their land.

I think of Chris Broughton bringing an AR-15 assault rifle to a health care reform rally in Phoenix [in 2009] and declaring, "We will forcefully resist people imposing their will on us through the strength of the majority with a vote."

These are some of the people who we'd be counting on to live peacefully among their fellow human beings in an anarchy? And we'd expect them to embrace an egalitarian—and possibly collectivized—society?

There are more than 250 million privately held firearms in the United States. That's no recipe for a peaceful society even *with* the rule of law intact.

Anarchy and Guns

During my ten years in the gun control movement, I've been struck by how often gun rights activists argue for anarchy.

Time and time again, they will say that gun control is a bad idea because "criminals don't obey laws." The inference is that laws only punish law-abiding citizens and, therefore, there is no use for them. Simultaneously, the gun lobby advocates for "Shoot First" laws in state legislatures across the country. These laws remove the common-law duty to retreat, allow individuals to use lethal force if they *subjectively* believe they are under fear of great bodily harm, and exempt shooters from criminal prosecution and civil lawsuits. Finally, the National Rifle Association preaches that the Second Amendment provides individuals with the right to stockpile firearms against our government and overthrow it violently should it become "tyrannical" (Google "tyranny" and see how many hits you get about the [Barack] Obama administration).

What would anarchy look like in the United States? Think *The Turner Diaries*, neo-Nazi William Luther Pierce's ultraviolent novel about the overthrow of the federal government by a small far right-wing network. The network's revolution is predicated on brutality and eventually leads to global nuclear war and the extermination of all Jews and nonwhites. The book's narrator has the following to say:

> Liberalism is an essentially feminine, submissive worldview. Perhaps a better adjective then feminine is infantile. It is the worldview of men who do not have the moral toughness, the spiritual strength to stand up and do singled combat with life, who cannot adjust to the reality that the world is not a huge, pink-and-blue, padded nursery in which the lions lie down with the lambs and everyone lives happily ever after. Nor should spiritually healthy men of our race even *want* to be like that, if it could be so.

The Turner Diaries was Timothy McVeigh's "Bible."[1] And it can be found at any gun show you walk into in America today.

1. Timothy McVeigh blew up a federal building in Oklahoma City in 1995, killing 168 people.

A democratic form of government inevitably produces some of the state-sanctioned violence that pacifists so abhor. But it also provides citizens with an elaborate set of mechanisms to influence policy and seek redress for injury. There are no such guarantees in a condition of anarchy.

Dr. Martin Luther King Jr. said it best in a speech in which he called for federal intervention to protect the lives of African Americans from mob violence: "It may be true that morality cannot be legislated, but behavior can be regulated. It may be true that the law cannot make a man love me, but it can keep him from lynching me, and I think that's pretty important." Amen.

The vision of anarcho-pacifists is noble and something we should aspire to—when civilization is finally ready to accommodate it. A famous admirer of Tolstoy's [Mahatma Gandhi] once put it thusly: "Representatives will become unnecessary if the national life becomes so perfect as to be self-controlled. It will then be a state of enlightened anarchy in which each person will become his own ruler. He will conduct himself in such a way that his behavior will not hamper the well-being of his neighbors. In an ideal state there will be no political institution and therefore no political power."

VIEWPOINT 5

> *"The army is an organisation whose most fundamental values cannot be brought in harmony with feminist values."*

Feminism and Pacifism Are Linked

Rachel Shabi

Rachel Shabi is a contributing writer to the Guardian *and the author of* Not the Enemy: Israel's Jews from Arab Lands. *In the following viewpoint, she reports on Idan Halili, a young woman who refused to serve in the Israeli military on feminist grounds. Shabi says that Halili believes feminism and militarism are incompatible because the army is hierarchical, its male culture encourages sexual harassment, and there is a link between militarism and domestic violence against women. Shabi concludes that Halili's protest raised awareness of the links between feminism and pacifism.*

As you read, consider the following questions:

1. According to Shabi, what are the two bases on which the Israeli conscience committees allow conscientious objection?

2. A 2003 survey showed that what percentage of women in the military experienced sexual harassment?
3. What is the organization Breaking the Silence, as the author describes?

Idan Halili, just 19-years-old, has written a feminist critique that has astounded established feminist voices around the world. Her analysis takes the form of a letter sent to the Israeli army asking for exemption from compulsory service, based on a feminist rejection of militarism. Last December [2005], having spent two weeks in military prison because of her refusal to serve, Halili was exempted from conscription; her views, she was told, deemed her "unsuitable".

Feminism Rejects Militarism

"The army is an organisation whose most fundamental values cannot be brought in harmony with feminist values," she wrote in her request for exemption. Halili argues that military service is incompatible with feminist ideology on several levels: because of a hierarchal, male-favouring army structure; because the army distorts gender roles; because of sexual harassment within the army; and because of an equation between military and domestic violence. Her arguments galvanised media attention in Israel, with Halili on prime-time TV news and bringing sidelined feminist arguments against militarism into the public arena for the first time.

Refusing to serve in the Israeli army is a cloudy, unpredictable process. Women's rights to conscientiously object were once set out by law. But in 2003, during the hearing that imprisoned five young men for refusing to serve on the "political" grounds of opposing the Israeli occupation, the court reinterpreted the exemption law for women, who now go through the same channels available to men. "Exemption from service is at the discretion of the minister of defence," says Yossi Wolfson, a lawyer with the feminist, anti-military group

New Profile. "But there is nothing mandatory and no specific procedure dictated by law." In practice, decisions are made by so-called "conscience committees", set up by the army drafting office, which allow conscientious objection [the refusal to serve in the military on grounds of conscience] only on the basis of religion or pacifism. "It's highly selective and tends to accept only a very radical, universal pacifism that holds all and any use of violence to be immoral," says Wolfson.

In Halili's case—as tends to happen—she was originally refused a hearing before a conscience committee and was sent to military prison when she refused to enlist. That decision was later reversed. "We argued that, although Halili's case against serving was 100% feminism, her ideology of feminism also meant she was a pacifist, objecting to any military system," says her solicitor, Smadar Ben-Natan.

The committee did not grant Halili exemption on the basis of conscientious objection. But the outcome was nonetheless some form of an indirect admission. "The committee said that her feminism, not pacifism, seemed more dominant and that, on the basis of holding such views, she would be unfit to serve," explains Ben-Natan.

The Army Is a Male Culture

Halili's success has overturned several assumptions—not least that a woman her age might have a coherent feminist ideology at all. A self-composed and swiftly eloquent woman from a kibbutz [collective community] in north Israel, Halili describes a long process of deliberation until "I understood that the army, in essence, does not square with feminist principles." Her feminist evolution, she says, involved a gradual linking of experiences, compounded by voluntary work with feminist organisations. It all led to "a difficult conflict between the notions on which I had been raised from an early age—according to which the military is a positive institution and serving

Sexual Harassment in the U.S. Military

Women are facing widespread sexual harassment and even rape by their male comrades in the military. The threat of sexual violence against female soldiers by their male colleagues is so great that women are warned not to go out to the bathroom alone at night. This has led women to stop drinking fluids at 3:00 in the afternoon and has even led to deaths due to dehydration.

How common are these problems? It is difficult to tell since the military has not published a complete survey, but indications are that 80% have faced sexual harassment and 30% have been raped.

Kevin Zeese,
"The Rape, Assault and Harassment of Women in the Military,"
Dissident Voice, *April 14, 2007. www.dissidentvoice.org.*

in it is a particularly respectable way of making your social contribution—and, on the other hand, feminist values of dignity and equality."

Halili's argument challenges the notion that Israeli women enjoy gender equality precisely because both sexes are conscripted. This goes beyond the assertion that a military social culture reveres the male "fighter" soldier while belittling the lesser, female role in the army (only 2% of women serve in combat units). Orna Sasson-Levy, professor in sociology and gender studies at Israel's Bar-Ilan University, says that the widely held assumption that female achievement in the Israeli army would translate to achievement in civil society has proved unfounded. Positions of high office in Israel are typically awarded to military achievers, which necessarily favours men who are able to attain a better status than women within the army. "Time and again, what I find in my research is that, even when the army is trying to create an equal-opportunity environment, the culture is so gendered, so masculine that women cannot achieve an equal place without completely co-operating with its chauvinistic structure and reproducing those in their behaviour towards other women."

This culture, among other things, is one of endemic sexual harassment. In 2003, research from the Israel Defence Force showed that a fifth of female soldiers experienced sexual harassment within the army. When the survey asked women about specific examples of harassment, such as humiliating innuendo or unwanted sexual proposals, that figure rose to 81% and 69% respectively. In other words, says Rela Mazali, one of the founders of New Profile, "Young women soldiers don't even know that what they are experiencing is called sexual harassment and they can do something about it." So female soldiers not only experience harassment, but are also conditioned not to view it as such.

The Military and Domestic Violence

Cynthia Enloe, professor of international development and women's studies at Clark University, has written extensively on gender and militarisation. She says, "UN [United Nations] and humanitarian workers in war zones now talk about the causal relationship between military and domestic violence—that is not a trivial understanding." Last year, researchers for the Haifa feminist centre, Isha L'Isha (woman to woman), found that, between 2000 and 2005, 47% of Israeli women murdered by their partners or relatives were killed by security guards, soldiers or police officers who carried licensed weapons. Sarai Aharoni, one of the researchers, reports that, during the same period, marked by numerous suicide attacks within Israel, "Female victims of domestic violence called help lines less—it seemed they felt it less legitimate when suicide bombings were taking place."

Testimonies from Breaking the Silence, an organisation of former soldiers describing injustices witnessed during military service, often relate feeling an apathy towards human life, an increased aggression and a loss of moral sensitivity as a result of serving in an occupying army. "All these patterns and behaviours are what we carry into civilian life," says Avichai Sharon, the organisation's spokesperson. Enloe reiterates this link: "The military doesn't like to admit that being trained as a special-forces trooper might endanger women when those same men come into a domestic setting."

Halili is now a volunteer with Israel's Hotline for Migrant Workers, in the area of sex trafficking. She is pleased just to have brought this issue of feminist anti-militarism into the public arena, but campaigners don't think that her case will necessarily provoke a flood of feminist appeals for exemption just yet. "I don't see women like Idan very often," says her solicitor, Ben-Natan. "She is exceptional".

VIEWPOINT 6

> *"Those endowed with estrogen who embrace pacifist or personal causes, such as women's rights or nuclear disarmament, don't become political leaders."*

Women Are Not More Likely to Be Pacifist than Men

Barbara Yaffe

Barbara Yaffe is a Canadian journalist and a political columnist for the Vancouver Sun. *In the following viewpoint, she argues that female political leaders are not more likely to be pacifist than men are. As evidence, she points to female leaders like Margaret Thatcher of Britain and Indira Gandhi of India, who did not pursue particularly peaceful policies. Yaffe argues that the process of becoming a political leader weeds out people who hold certain opinions. She concludes that more women in public office will probably not result in a more peaceful world.*

As you read, consider the following questions:

1. Who was Golda Meir, according to Yaffe?
2. What type of leaders do women who embrace pacifist or personal causes become, according to Yaffe?

Barbara Yaffe, "Column: Would the World Be More Peaceful with Women at the Helm?" *Vancouver Sun*, September 25, 2009. Reproduced by permission.

3. Who does Yaffe point to as an exception to the rule that female politicians do not pursue pacifist goals?

With the perennial push to boost the number of women in politics, it's worth asking whether the world would be a more peaceful place with a bigger proportion of females at the helm.

Women Rulers and Peace

The only way to go beyond the theoretical in responding to such a question is to scrutinize the records of those women who've ruled.

Women leaders, of course, are in the minority. But experience suggests a world of women presidents and prime ministers, queens and empresses would yield a world order not dissimilar to the one we have now.

Think Golda Meir, prime minister of Israel from 1969 to 1974, dubbed the Iron Lady of Israeli politics. A previous prime minister, David Ben-Gurion, labelled Meir "the best man in the government."

Meir had no qualms mobilizing her country's army to do battle in the Yom Kippur War.

Think of another Iron Lady, three-term British Prime Minister [PM] Margaret Thatcher, also known as the "Milk Snatcher". She sent British troops to the Falkland Islands in a war against Argentina in 1982.

For good measure, she supported retaining capital punishment in her country and opposed any relaxation of divorce laws.

Think German Chancellor Angela Merkel, dubbed the Iron Frau since her 2005 electoral win, who argued for Germany's nuclear power to be phased out less quickly than the previous government had planned.

Think Indian PM Indira Gandhi, who launched a national nuclear weapons program in 1967, and showed her authoritarian side by declaring a state of emergency in two Indian states in 1975.

Then, in 1984, Gandhi authorized troops to open fire in Amritsar's Golden Temple, which was besieged by Sikh extremists, resulting in significant civilian casualties.

Does anyone believe that, had Hillary Clinton become U.S. president, she'd have curtailed the current [2009] fighting in Afghanistan?

When a woman politician works her way through the political system and arrives at a leadership position, she indeed has had to work through "a system", one that usually is preexisting, mightily entrenched and inevitably male dominated.

Women, like men, get to the top by way of a no-holds-barred political process and those without the perceived necessary skills don't make it.

The System Is More Important than the Gender

Like their male counterparts, women aspirants must glean support from mostly male partisans, make deals, issue IOUs ["I owe you" agreements], possibly compromise personal beliefs.

And once at the pinnacle, events tend to dictate action. Elected leaders respond to circumstances that arise knowing they need to carefully heed both their party hierarchies and voters—not their private whims and preferences.

For Meir that meant an unavoidable war with Syria. For Pakistani's Benazir Bhutto, in the late nineties, that meant providing military and financial support for the Taliban (as did the U.S. at that time).

Circumstances do not often permit women leaders to exhibit a softer side. This is not motherhood these women are undertaking, it's leadership.

Linking Feminism and Pacifism Undermines Peace

Many feminists have long rejected the argument of women's inherent pacifism as problematic and counter-productive. Yet, this notion has noticeably resurfaced [as of 2009] within the current literature on women in conflict and peace building.... Feminists writing within these areas have represented women as mythical peace builders and romanticised their contributions to peace. They have also overemphasised the existence of a common, feminist, socialist, pacifist agenda and overstated accounts of women's victimisation at the hands of violent and bellicose masculinity. The persistence of such concepts arguably reinforces the hierarchical gender dichotomies regarding masculinity and femininity and as such sustains militarism, violence against women, inequality and the exclusion of women from the area of peace and security.

This [viewpoint critiques] examples of current literature where the stereotype of feminist pacifism is to be found and explore[s] some of the reasons behind the continued adherence to such idea.... If we disconnect femininity from peace we would dismantle a major source of militarism. Deconstructing the stereotypes surrounding femininity and masculinity and the rejection of all kinds of biological explanations for gender behavioural differences in war and peace are necessary conditions for achieving equality and possibly peace.

Sahla Aroussi,
"Women, Peace and Security: Moving Beyond Feminist Pacifism," Political Studies Association, May 2009. www.psa.ac.uk.journals.

Those endowed with estrogen who embrace pacifist or personal causes, such as women's rights or nuclear disarmament, don't become political leaders. They become leaders of national nongovernmental organizations.

Accordingly, journalist Gloria Steinem, preoccupied with seeking justice for women, co-founded the U.S. Women's Action Alliance, the Coalition of Labor Union Women, the Women's Media Center and Choice USA.

Australian anti-nuclear campaigner Helen Caldicott became founder of Women's Action for New Directions.

Just look around. At this juncture, there's nothing about actions taken by Michelle Bachelet, Chile's first female president and a single mother, to suggest her gender.

And certainly, former Alaska Governor Sarah Palin, a possible presidential aspirant, doesn't present herself as a feminist who'd promote pacifist strategies.

Nor do any of the women on [Canadian Prime Minister] Stephen Harper's front bench, for that matter. They all followed the party line when it came to voting to keep troops in Afghanistan.

Of course exceptions can always be found, like New Zealand's Prime Minister Helen Clark who has helped push her country to be nuclear free.

But for the most part the notion that more women political leaders would nurture a more peaceful world is no more than wishful thinking.

What do Canadian women who've been or are MPs [members of Parliament] think?

Libby Davies: "I've always believed that a critical mass of progressive women in leadership roles, whether in government, the workplace, or internationally, would be transforming. Our priority is improving the quality of life, not destroying it."

Pat Carney: A more peaceful world? "Not unless stereotyping changes, and women start receiving credit for their contribution." Carney suggests the world should give the idea a try—elect more female leaders—and find out.

Deborah Grey: "Women are, generally, nurturers and consensus builders. We are also more emotional by nature. [But] sadly, I do not think a 'magic pill' of more women leaders would result in a more peaceful world."

Periodical and Internet Sources Bibliography

The following articles have been selected to supplement the diverse views presented in this chapter.

Florence and William Boos	"Pacifism and the Arguments Against War," Iowa Green Party, March 5, 2003. www.greens.org.
Bryan Caplan	"Why Libertarians Should Be Pacifists, Not Isolationists," *EconLog* (blog), March 22, 2010. http://econlog.econlib.org.
Jason Justice	"Defining Anarchism," Lucy Parsons Project, June 2003. www.lucyparsonsproject.org.
Jason Laning	"In Defense of Anarchism: What Kind of Peace Does Government Provide?" Waging Nonviolence, January 4, 2010. http://wagingnonviolence.org.
Bennett Muraskin	"Secular Jews and Pacifism," *Secular Culture & Ideas*, 2007. www.jbooks.com.
George Orwell	"Pacifism and the War," *Partisan Review*, August–September 1942.
Charley Reese	"It's Common Sense, Not Pacifism," AntiWar.com, December 22, 2007. www.antiwar.com.
Rosemary Radford Ruether	"Feminism Must Rediscover Pacifist Roots," *National Catholic Reporter*, December 20, 2002.
Roman Shusterman	"Secular Pacifism," *Humanitarian Socialist Party* (blog), November 13, 2009. http://nopolicestatecoalition.blogspot.com.

OPPOSING VIEWPOINTS® SERIES

Chapter 4

What Is the Link Between Pacifism and Political and Social Issues?

Chapter Preface

One of the most important political and social questions facing pacifists is the question of conscientious objection. Conscientious objectors (COs) are people who refuse to go to war because of pacifist convictions. In some situations, certain people may be legally granted CO status. In other cases, COs may face legal prosecution.

The recognition of CO status has a long history in the United States. In the colonial era, members of historic peace churches—especially the Mennonites, Quakers, and the Church of the Brethren—were granted exemptions from militia service. The United States instituted its first draft during the Civil War, and at that time, again, COs were recognized, though they sometimes had to pay a fee to escape military service. In World War I, the government became more restrictive and jailed hundreds of Americans who claimed CO status. "By World War II, the government had created a program of 'alternative civilian service' to provide conscientious objectors with noncombatant support roles" such as in hospitals or parks, according to an August 24, 2007, article on the NOW on PBS website.

Conscientious objection is usually seen as an individual act of conscience. However, at times it has blurred into or touched upon broader opposition to particular wars. Thus, according to an article on the website of the Peace Abbey, "During the Vietnam War more than 170,000 men were officially recognized as conscientious objectors. Thousands of other young men resisted the draft by burning their draft cards, serving jail sentences, or leaving the country. Though the military is currently an all-volunteer organization, when the [Persian] Gulf War broke out in 1991, twenty-five hundred men and women volunteers serving in the US armed forces refused to serve in Saudi Arabia on the basis of conscience. While draft opposition has been an individual decision made by a minority in all US wars, public opposition to wars such as the War of 1812, the Mexican[-American] War, World War I, and the Vietnam War sparked mass movements that reached far beyond men of draft age."

To obtain conscientious objector status, a person must be "opposed to serving in the armed forces and/or bearing arms on the grounds of moral or religious principles," according to an April 30, 2002, article on the Selective Service System US government website. The website also notes that the objection to war must not be based on "politics, expediency, or self-interest," which effectively means that the person's objection must be to all wars, rather than to a particular war. The website also explains that once a person makes a claim for CO status, he "is required to appear before his local board to explain his beliefs." The board then rules whether the person may be exempt from the draft.

The following viewpoints examine other ways in which pacifism may affect or be affected by political or social issues.

Viewpoint 1

> *"The underlying principle . . . of the movement opposing abortion is a commitment to life and a renewal of the commitment to nonviolence that characterized the first Christian disciples."*

The Pro-Life Movement and Nonviolence Are Linked

James R. Kelly

James R. Kelly is a professor emeritus of sociology at Fordham University in New York City and a member of University Faculty for Life. In the following viewpoint, he argues that the pro-life movement should be rooted in an ethic of nonviolence and peace. He suggests that the pro-life movement should distance itself from conservative politics and should instead commit itself to a range of peace issues such as embracing pacifism, organizing against the death penalty, and opposing abortion.

As you read, consider the following questions:

1. Why did the magazine *Sojourners* say that it had initially failed to oppose abortion?

James R. Kelly, "Finding Renewal," *America Magazine*, February 16, 2009. Reproduced by permission.

2. The National Conference of Catholic Bishops taught that the same moral principle governed which two traditional church prohibitions?

3. According to Kelly, why is the Consistent Life network mostly invisible to popular opinion?

The catalyst for the following reflections was an Internet exchange during the [Barack] Obama-[John] McCain presidential election campaign [of 2008] with a long-term activist member of University Faculty for Life. He was disappointed that priests in their Sunday homilies rarely spoke about abortion but frequently preached about other issues of public policy like war, immigration and poverty. I responded by asking, "Won't our children, our grandchildren and historians want to know what the pro-life movement said about the wars in Iraq and Afghanistan and nuclear disarmament?" His response: "Like other civil rights movements, I think they will. . . . Of course, all this is predicated on our having a pro-life movement to write about."

Is Pro-Life Similar to the Pacifist Movement?

His answer prompted me to consider a larger problem: What kind of movement is the pro-life movement? Is the campaign against abortion more like the movement for civil rights or the movement for nonviolence? This question transcends the 2008 election and the elections that will follow. It is much more than a conceptual question of definition. The answer will have very practical consequences. How we understand the nature of the pro-life movement will determine not only strategy, tactics and voting decisions, but also how pro-life advocates view the inevitable setbacks and defeats as well as the long-term, eschatological significance of their efforts.

To persevere in an enduring pro-life campaign, we must retrieve the contemporary origin of the movement opposing abortion and regain its initiating charism. The movement can do this by explicitly recognizing its three-part history: (1) the radical beginnings of some of the opposition to abortion; (2) the tactical and temporary political co-option of moral conservatives by fiscal conservatives, a linkage probably definitively eroded by the last election [of 2008, in which Republicans were defeated]; and (3) the retrieval of the movement's core radicalism, which located opposition to abortion within the nonviolence movement, itself the principled core of the peace movement. In other words, we must grasp why the movement always found unfair the name "anti-abortion" (much less "anti-choice"), why it merely accepted the term "right-to-life" but always instinctively chose to define itself as "pro-life."

The fundamental insight, that objections to abortion and objections to war are rooted in the same moral principles, was present at the very beginning of the modern anti-abortion movement. In 1964, almost a decade before *Roe v. Wade* [a Supreme Court decision that legalized abortion], Tom Cornell, one of the founders of the Catholic Peace Fellowship, said that it was pacifism that brought him to protest both the Vietnam War and abortion. "Catholic pacifists," he explained, "are opposed to war because it is the planned, mass taking of human life for political purposes . . . [and] we are opposed to abortion, euthanasia, capital punishment, and economically enforced starvation also, on the same basis."

Two years before *Roe v. Wade*, Gordon Zahn, one of the founders of Pax Christi, an international Catholic peace organization formed after World War II, linked opposing abortion and opposing war: "It is not just a matter of consistency; in a very real sense it is the choice between integrity and hypocrisy. No one who publicly mourns the senseless burning of a napalmed child should be indifferent to the intentional killing of a living fetus in the womb. . . ."

In 1973, the year the Supreme Court, by its 7-to-2 decision in *Roe v. Wade*, struck down all state laws prohibiting or restricting abortion, the first college organization was formed in the abortion controversy: the National Youth Pro-Life Coalition at the University of Minnesota. It linked opposition to abortion and opposition to the Vietnam War. "The Coalition is deeply concerned that our contemporary society is not consistent in its respect for human life," a student founder, Susan Hilgers, said in an interview, and challenged those who were "anti-abortion, pro-war and pro-capital punishment" to greater moral consistency, because "true conservatism should involve a willingness to 'conserve' all human life."

Six years later, Juli Loesch organized Pro-lifers for Survival, which also linked opposition to war and opposition to abortion. In 1980 *Sojourners*, an evangelical Christian journal, explicitly connected opposition to abortion to its long-standing opposition to the arms race and to capital punishment. The editors explained that from the start, moral consistency had required their opposition to abortion, and that their earlier failure to oppose abortion publicly was prompted by their distaste for some of the tactics of the anti-abortion movement. They added, "The truth is that many poor women do not regard abortion as a real solution but as a brutal substitute for social justice and even as white society's way of controlling the population of racial minorities."

Consistent Ethic of Life

While the notion of "a consistent ethic of life" had originally emerged among groups of religiously committed pacifists, who intuitively saw a connection between their moral abhorrence of war and abortion, the phrase entered more mainstream discourse in the aftermath of the late Cardinal Joseph Bernardin's Gannon lecture at Fordham University on Dec. 6, 1983, entitled "A Consistent Ethic of Life: An American Catholic Dialogue." Cardinal Bernardin had been invited to speak on the U.S. bishops' recently published pastoral letter on the morality of nuclear weapons, *The Challenge of Peace*. The letter had received considerable attention in the broader American community, provoking a variety of responses.

His audience and the journalists present expected the cardinal to address the letter's criticism of the [Ronald] Reagan administration's expansionist military policies and its doctrine of mutually assured destruction as a defense against nuclear war. But Cardinal Bernardin surprised his audience by announcing that his talk would be about abortion in the context of the church's evolving teaching about war and peace. For three reasons the surprise that greeted his announcement revealed how far the protest movement against abortion had strayed from its original moral intuitions and how it had become associated with political conservatism. The surprise of the audience and the journalists present was itself surprising, given the history of the anti-abortion movement.

First, the Second Vatican Council [of 1962–1965, which reformulated many church doctrines] in its "Pastoral Constitution on the Church in the Modern World" (1964) included abortion not as a single issue but as the third item in a list of 16 examples of violence against human life.

Second, when in accord with Vatican II the U.S. bishops inaugurated their Respect Life program in the year before *Roe v. Wade*, they invited Catholics and others to focus on the "sanctity of life and the many threats to life in the modern world, including violence, hunger and poverty."

Third, just seven months before the cardinal's lecture at Fordham, the National Conference of Catholic Bishops [currently known as the U.S. Conference of Catholic Bishops] in their pastoral letter *The Challenge of Peace* taught that the same moral principle governed both the traditional just war[1] prohibition against the direct targeting of civilians and the

1. Just war is a theological tradition that provides criteria for entering into and conducting wars.

traditional prohibition against abortion. "Nothing," the bishops taught, "can justify a direct attack on innocent human life, in or out of warfare. Abortion is precisely such an attack." The bishops acknowledged that the consistency they found in the Catholic moral tradition linking war and abortion was not widely known and accepted, even by Catholics.

In his Fordham address Cardinal Bernardin confirmed this traditional and contemporary moral teaching that abortion and military violence directed at civilians were immoral for the same reason. Following the orientation of the Second Vatican Council, he situated opposition to abortion in the context of helping the vulnerable: "If one contends, as we do, that the right of every fetus to be born should be protected by civil law and supported by civil consensus, then our moral, political and economic responsibilities do not stop at the moment of birth. Those who defend the right to life of the weakest among us must be equally visible in support of the quality of life of the powerless among us: the old and the young, the hungry and the homeless, the undocumented immigrant and the unemployed worker. Such a quality of life posture translates into specific political and economic positions on tax policy, employment generation, welfare policy, nutrition and feeding programs and health care. Consistency means we cannot have it both ways. We cannot urge a compassionate society and vigorous public policy to protect the rights of the unborn and then argue that compassion and significant public programs on behalf of the needy undermine the moral fiber of the society or are beyond the proper scope of governmental responsibility."

As had the National Conference of Catholic Bishops before him, Cardinal Bernardin acknowledged: "We should begin with the honest recognition that the shaping of a consensus among Catholics on the spectrum of life issues is far from finished and that we face the challenge of stating our case, which is shaped in terms of our faith and our religious con-

A Quaker on Nonviolence and Abortion

If the fetus is a human child, to my mind the pro-life case is made on the basis of the insights of nonviolence and the testimony on human equality [the Quaker belief that all people are spiritually equal]. With this difference in mind, it was in fact disheartening to me how many people simply went along with my characterization of abortion as child-killing and found it justified anyway.

Rachel MacNair,
"My Personal Journey on the Abortion Issue,"
Friends Journal, *February 2010. www.friendsjournal.org.*

victions, in nonreligious terms which others of different faith convictions might find morally persuasive."

Adhering to Principle

Despite a lack of public notice, by the mid-1980s there existed a wide and dense network of groups committed to nonviolence; these groups applied the traditional moral principle underlying their rejection of modern warfare to abortion. At the last gathering of Pro-lifers for Survival in March 1987, a Seamless Garment Network was formed. Its mission statement reads: "We the undersigned are committed to the protection of life, which is threatened in today's world by war, abortion, poverty, racism, the arms race, the death penalty, and euthanasia. We believe that these issues are linked under a consistent ethic of life. We challenge those working on all or some of these issues to maintain a cooperative spirit of peace, reconciliation, and respect in protecting the unprotected."

By 2003 the network had over 120 member organizations, most of them with religious identities, such as Catholic Worker groups and diocesan peace and justice committees, Pax Christi, Evangelicals for Social Action, Sojourners and the Buddhist Vihara Society. Because the seamless-garment metaphor required constant explication in a secular society, the network now identifies itself as Consistent Life—an international network for peace, justice and life. In efforts to overcome media stereotypes of abortion opponents, Consistent Life has taken out advertisements in publications explaining the consistent ethic of life. Signers have included such prominent peace activists as Daniel Berrigan, S.J., Elizabeth McAlister and the late Philip Berrigan, Jim and Shelley Douglass, Joan Chittister, O.S.B., the late Eileen Egan, Jean Goss and Hildegard Goss-Mayr of the International Fellowship of Reconciliation; Bishops Thomas Gumbleton, Walter F. Sullivan and Raymond G. Hunthausen; the Nobel prize recipients Mairead Corrigan-Maguire and Adolfo Pérez Esquivel; and the high-profile theologians Harvey Cox and Stanley Hauerwas.

The Consistent Life network is mostly invisible to popular opinion, because the principle of nonviolence itself is neither recognized nor appreciated in American popular culture. Instances of particular protest against particular wars will receive attention in the media, but not the fundamental principle of pacifism—namely, the commitment to nonviolence. Indeed, no term and no principle is more alien to the nation-state, especially in its foreign affairs, than nonviolence. Groups committed to nonviolence must mute and marginalize their radical principles in order to gain entry to the world of public opinion and commentary. Even in the churches, the early and strong biblical traditions showing that Christ taught nonviolence and his followers accepted it have been mostly marginalized.

Strategies for the Future

To unlink opposition to abortion from the center of the Republican Party establishment would mean, among other things, that the pro-life movement would become freer to renew its original moral intuition. In doing so, the movement would become more widely recognized and morally respected as promoting a consistent ethic of life. Such an ethic, based on the biblical values of nonviolence and equality, challenges all major and minor streams of American politics.

The *telos*—the underlying principle, the driving force and ultimate goal—of the movement opposing abortion is a commitment to life and a renewal of the commitment to nonviolence that characterized the first Christian disciples and many others after them. The 2008 election and its aftermath could prove to be the occasion for a pro-life return to its deepest moral insight: that a resort to violence in any dimension is a negation of the human good.

Viewpoint 2

"As a Christian, feminist Quaker I cannot abide any national policy that has the effect of controlling women's lives. That is not my Peace Testimony."

The Pro-Life Movement Is Not Linked to Nonviolence

Guli Fager

Guli Fager works as healthy sexuality education coordinator at the University of Texas at Austin and blogs about sex and sexual health under the name Julie Sunday. In the following viewpoint, she argues that the pro-life movement is not based on nonviolence. Instead, she says, it is dedicated to forcing women into traditional roles where they can be controlled by men. She suggests that Quakers and those who support peace should work to reduce the violence against women that results in the need for abortion.

As you read, consider the following questions:

1. What is the March for Life, in the author's view?

2. What does Fager say that abstinence-only sex educators mean when they claim to want to change the culture around sex?
3. Since *Roe v. Wade*, what does Fager say has increased and what has decreased?

This January [2010] I was in Washington, D.C., just after the March for Life, which annually mourns the *Roe v. Wade* decision [a Supreme Court decision that legalized abortion in the United States]. While near the Capitol I came upon a leaflet on the ground that reminded me perfectly why, as a sex educator, a Christian, a feminist, and a Quaker [a historically peaceful church], I still vehemently support, advocate, and fight for the right to abortion for women who need it.

Pro-Life Seeks to Restrict Women

The leaflet, "An Appeal for Insistence," is a tri-fold from the organization the American Society for the Defense of Tradition, Family and Property that goes by the acronym TFP:

> Thus, pro-abortion radicals understand all too well what is at stake. Take abortion away and the whole edifice of the sexual revolution comes crashing to the ground. Loose permissive relationships will no longer be possible. People will be forced to deal with their sexuality in the manner which nature prescribes—namely traditional marriage.

It is my belief that the people like [Quaker feminist pro-life advocate Rachel] MacNair who earnestly believe that abortion is an unacceptable violence are being used by groups whose real goal—as frankly stated in the above quote and echoed by other, far more mainstream organizations such as Focus on the Family—is to undo the sexual revolution and return women in the U.S., who have enjoyed greater social gains in the last 50 years than ever in history, to a system in which unintended pregnancy is a dire consequence of nonmarital sex and the only acceptable place for women is as wives of men.

For some women unintended pregnancy continues to be such a punishment. Women in the United States, particularly those who are poor, still do not have universal access to contraceptive and other health services that could prevent pregnancy and thereby render abortion mostly unnecessary. As a sex educator, 95 percent of the work I do is focused around preventing unwanted outcomes from sex—pregnancy, sexually transmitted infections, assault, etc.—but abortion is always there, a specter on the horizon, the nuclear option for when all else fails.

In Texas, where I work as a sex educator at the state's flagship university, I daily encounter the sinister effects of abstinence-only "education" programs, which, by the way, are also produced by organizations whose explicit goals are to reverse the sexual revolution and the gains women have made as a result, hiding behind such language as "changing the culture" around sex. Friends, what they mean when they say "change the culture" is to return us to a time when unwed women who became pregnant had three choices: shotgun marriage; social banishment; or dangerous, illegal abortion. I have read too many stories of back-alley procedures and young women sent away to "maternity homes" where, at the end of their pregnancies, they would be sedated, restrained, and their newborn babies taken from them before they ever had a chance to see him or her, to cede an inch to that kind of talk. If that is the "culture change" that pro-life organizations want, then, to paraphrase the famously pro-life [conservative politician] Sarah Palin, "Thanks but no thanks."

Pro-Life Does Not Reduce Violence

The student body at the university where I work is more than 50 percent female. Increasing numbers of professional schools, including law and medical schools, are more than half women. The opportunities now available to women exist precisely because women can control their fertility. Access to contraceptives—and, for some, abortion—is essential to women's equality and a basic human right.

As a Christian, feminist Quaker I cannot abide any national policy that has the effect of controlling women's lives. That is not my Peace Testimony. MacNair may not realize this, but the men behind the curtain on this issue want to control women and their sexuality. Since *Roe v. Wade*, use of contraception has increased, and abortion, unplanned pregnancy, and rape have all decreased. Allowing women to control their own bodies gives them agency, and the changing indicators above prove that things for women are better when we are in charge.

Susan B. Anthony, a Quaker feminist routinely valorized by Feminists for Life, with which MacNair is also associated, said the following in her speech "Social Purity," in 1875: "The work of woman is not to lessen the severity or the certainty of the penalty for violation of the moral law [referring to abortion and infanticide], but to prevent this violation by the removal of the causes which lead to it."

My query to MacNair . . . is: What are we, as Friends [that is, as Quakers, also known as the Religious Society of Friends], doing to remove the social and systemic violence women face that denies them vital options and as a result forces them to turn to abortion? Efforts to re-criminalize abortion will not "protect innocent life" and that is not their goal; they trap and punish women who dare to set and achieve goals outside of the framework of "traditional marriage."

Anthony, as well as [Quaker feminist] Lucretia Mott and many of our Quaker foremothers before them, fought long and hard for women to have the opportunities we have today. Contraception and abortion are a part of the picture. We cannot stop abortion but we, as Friends, can work to reduce women's need for it by advocating for comprehensive sex education, universal access to health care that includes contraceptives, and teaching our own youth. I agree with Anthony and [social activist Elizabeth Cady] Stanton about our work, and we have it cut out for us—but it is not only the work of women; it is the work of all Friends.

Viewpoint 3

"If we were to bring Paul into our current dialogue about whether Christians should support the use of torture, his response would be a resolute 'No!'"

Pacifism Should Lead Christians to Oppose Torture

V. Henry T. Nguyen

V. Henry T. Nguyen is an adjunct lecturer in theological studies at Loyola Marymount University. In the following viewpoint, he argues that Paul's words in the Bible reject the use of violence and torture. Nguyen says that Paul argues against violence and that Christians need to identify with the crucified, not the crucifier. Therefore, Nguyen concludes, the violent war on terror, and the use of torture in pursuit of it, are not theologically consistent with Christianity.

As you read, consider the following questions:

1. Why does Sarah Sentilles suggest that some Christian communities may view torture as salvific, necessary, and justified?

2. Who does Nguyen say provides the earliest interpretation of the crucified Christ?
3. Who is Richard Hays, and what does he believe is Paul's attitude toward violence?

The recent Pew [Research Center] findings—that churchgoers, especially white evangelical Protestants, are more likely to believe that torture can be justified—have caused many commentators to wonder whether particular forms of Christian theology engender an acceptance of the use of torture.

Paul Would Not Support Torture

In a recent article on *Religion Dispatches*, Sarah Sentilles suggests that Christian theologies and images of Christ's crucifixion (essentially is an act of torture) have influenced some Christian communities' understanding of torture as salvific, necessary, and justified. This view of torture is especially fueled by what is known as atonement theology: the view that Jesus's death provided reparation for humanity's sins against God.

So what would a Christian theological response against torture look like?

Most Christian theologies are rooted in the writings of Paul, who is particularly celebrated this year [2009] by the Catholic Church on the bimillenial anniversary of the apostle's birth; Paul provides the earliest interpretation of the meaning of the crucified Christ. People often forget, or are not aware, that nowhere in the gospels does Jesus himself explain the meaning of his own suffering on the cross. But Paul does.

And I believe that if we were to bring Paul into our current dialogue about whether Christians should support the use of torture, his response would be a resolute "No!"

First, Paul's life experiences reflect a radical shift from violence to nonviolence due to his Christian conversion. The Acts of the Apostles describes Paul before his conversion as persecuting the earliest followers of Christ. At the outset of a religiously sanctioned campaign to persecute Christians in Damascus, Paul encounters the risen Christ on the road to Damascus and undergoes a dramatic, religious conversion; from persecutor to preacher. Paul's encounter with Christ, then, transformed his life of religious violence to a life of love.

When we shift our attention to Paul's writings, we see further indications of his stance on nonviolence. Take, for instance, his statements in Romans, which echo the themes of nonviolence and non-retaliation in Jesus's Sermon on the Mount:

> Bless those who persecute you; bless and do not curse them. . . . Live in harmony with one another. . . . Do not repay anyone evil for evil, but take thought for what is noble in the sight of all. If it is possible, so far as it depends on you, live peaceably with all. Beloved, never avenge yourselves, but leave room for the wrath of God; for it is written, "Vengeance is mine, I will repay, says the Lord." No, "if your enemies are hungry, feed them; if they are thirsty, give them something to drink; for by doing this you will heap burning coals on their heads." Do not be overcome by evil, but overcome evil with good.

Not to Crucify but to Be Crucified

Scholars have typically paid little attention to the themes of nonviolence in Paul's letters, and some would argue that Paul does not hold such a position. In recent times, however, a small voice in biblical studies has drawn attention to Paul's theme of nonviolence as it relates to his understanding of God's restorative justice. New Testament scholar Richard Hays asserts in *The Moral Vision of the New Testament: Community, Cross, New Creation*, "There is not a syllable in the Pauline letters that can be cited in support of Christians employing violence." He further explains that even in cases where Paul employs military imagery in his rhetoric, they "actually have the

The American Church Has Abandoned Christ by Supporting Torture

[Jesus] founded an international, countercultural movement . . . to advance the peaceable and just reign of [His] Father in this rebellious world. We American Christians have turned it into a culture-religion that has nothing to say even about, say, waterboarding, slamming people repeatedly into walls, forced nudity, prolonged shackling, 11 days of sleep deprivation, psychological terror, sexual humiliation, . . . and so much more!

David Gushee, "Opinion: A Christian's Lament over the Pew Torture Poll," Associated Baptist Press, May 5, 2009. www.abpnews.com.

opposite effect: the warfare imagery is drafted into the service of the gospel, rather than the reverse." We observe Paul, then, as actually re-visioning violence in light of the gospel.

We see in the life and teachings of Paul an inculcation of a Christian lifestyle of justice and nonviolence through the cross; one that imitates the crucified Christ who did not inflict suffering on others, but who embraced it for the sake of others. [New Testament scholar] Michael Gorman, in his book *Reading Paul*, argues that the saving, restorative justice of God "takes place not by inflicting violence on the enemy, but by absorbing violence on behalf of the enemy. Its extreme modus operandi is not to crucify but to be crucified. It does not require the destruction of the enemy but the embrace of the enemy."

I believe that Christians must embrace and embody Paul's revision of violence. This also needs to be applied to our understanding of America's rhetoric and activities of justified war and violence, and the "war on terror." We must be mindful that Christians are to embody the cruciform ethics of not crucifying (i.e., torturing) one's enemy, but to be crucified (i.e., be tortured) on behalf of one's enemy. And our attention needs to be not only on those who are tortured, but perhaps even more so on those who torture.

Rhetoric such as a "war on terror" that seeks to eliminate terrorism and condones the use of violence and torture (i.e., terror) is contrary to Paul's view of God's peaceable, restorative justice.

As Gorman argues in his newest book, *Inhabiting the Cruciform God: Kenosis, Justification, and Theosis in Paul's Narrative Soteriology*:

> That world leaders who call themselves practicing Christians (or Muslims or Jews) seem to espouse such views and that many others who follow such leaders seem prepared to carry out their allegedly sacred violence without question should concern us deeply. More specifically, as an alternative to this kind of thinking and acting, the church of Jesus Christ must make nonviolence a more central dimension of its life and teaching and a central corollary of its creedal affirmation that God raised the crucified Jesus from the dead, thereby ending the case for violence as the modus operandi of God and of God's people in the world.

Nonviolent Reconciliation

Those who are in Christ today, with Paul, identify with the life-giving and reconciling cross of Christ, validated by God in the resurrection, not as an expression of a violent personality or a conviction that violence can be sacred and salutary, but in the paradoxical belief that in Christ and his cross God was nonviolently reconciling the world to himself and giving to us the ongoing task of nonviolent reconciliation of people to God and to one another. In that spirit, we may need to be prepared to absorb violence, but not to inflict it. Such is one central aspect of the calling of our time to those justified, sanctified, and divinized in Christ.

In sum, Paul's stance on nonviolent reconciliation and justice provides us with the necessary anti-torture posture for Christians today as they reflect on and respond to the pressing issues of war, terrorism, and torture.

Will Christians embrace Paul's moral vision and lifestyle of justice and nonviolence?

VIEWPOINT 4

> *"The bizarre claim that those who oppose torture . . . are not just pacifists, but* radical *pacifists . . . is so patently ridiculous that no one can truly believe it."*

Even Those Who Are Not Pacifists Should Oppose Torture

Joe Carter

Joe Carter is the Web editor of First Things, *an inter-denomination Christian journal. In the following viewpoint, he responds to the charge that those who oppose torture are radical pacifists. He points out that many respected military veterans and officers oppose torture, and he argues that the Christian faith demands opposition to torture. He maintains that those who support torture are promoting pagan values. He concludes that the acceptance of torture is a sign of the debasement of conservatism and the marginalization of true Christian perspectives.*

As you read, consider the following questions:

1. Who are Joseph Hoar and John Hutson, and what is their position on torture, according to Carter?

Joe Carter, "Do Only Radical Pacifists Oppose Torture?" *First Things*, January 4, 2010. Reproduced by permission.

2. What interrogation tool does Carter say was used in the most successful interrogation of an al Qaeda operative?

3. What is the immoral purpose that Russell Saltzman says torture serves?

> To do evil a human being must first of all believe that what he's doing is good. . . . Ideology—that is what gives evildoing its long-sought justification and gives the evildoer the necessary steadfastness and determination. That is the social theory which helps to make his acts seem good instead of bad in his own and others' eyes, so that he won't hear reproaches and curses but will receive praise and honors. That was how the agents of the Inquisition fortified their wills: by invoking Christianity; the conquerors of foreign lands, by extolling the grandeur of their Motherland; the colonizers, by civilization; the Nazis, by race, and the Jacobins (early and late), by equality, brotherhood, and the happiness of future generations.
>
> —*Aleksandr Solzhenitsyn,* The Gulag Archipelago

To this list Solzhenitsyn could add American conservatism: The movement is increasingly becoming a pagan-influenced ideology, providing long-sought justification for evildoing and providing us the steadfastness and determination to do what we know is wrong and the boldness to call evil good.

Opposition to Waterboarding Is Not Pacifism

How else can we explain the willingness of conservatives to not only defend the intrinsically evil act of torture but to also claim that those who oppose such evil have no place in making decisions about war and peace?

That is the jaw-dropping position advanced by Marc [A.] Thiessen [a former White House and Department of Defense speechwriter] in (of all places) *National Review Online*:

> Jonah [Goldberg] is absolutely right that opposition to waterboarding [an interrogation technique involving controlled drowning] is an honorable position—but it's a little more like pacifism than opposition to the death penalty. As I explain in *Courting Disaster* [Thiessen's book], the evidence is overwhelming that waterboarding helped stop a number of terrorist attacks. Which means if you oppose waterboarding in all circumstances, it means you are willing to accept as the price another terrorist attack.
>
> [. . .]
>
> Those who argue that we should not use enhanced techniques even on the KSM's [terrorists like Khalid Sheikh Mohammed] of the world are effectively arguing from a position of radical pacifism. They are opposed to coercion no matter what the cost in innocent lives. We should respect their opinion, the way we respect the right of conscientious objectors to abstain from military service. But that does not mean we put pacifists in charge of decisions on war and peace. Same should go for decisions when it comes to interrogation.

It's difficult to know where to begin on such an embarrassing argument. Let's start with the bizarre claim that those who oppose torture, specifically in the form of waterboarding, are not just pacifists, but *radical* pacifists. Such a claim is so patently ridiculous that no one can truly believe it. Indeed, I suspect that even Mr. Thiessen doesn't really believe his own insult.

Could he truly believe that people like me (a fifteen-year Marine Corps veteran) and Sen. John McCain [a Vietnam veteran] ("Waterboarding is torture") are radical pacifists? What about Gen. Charles Krulak, former commandant of the Marine Corps, and Joseph Hoar, former commander in chief of U.S. Central Command, who claim that waterboarding is torture and note that such methods "have nurtured the recuperative power of the enemy." Or what about John Hutson, former

An Account of Being Waterboarded

You may have read by now the official lie about this treatment [waterboarding], which is that it "simulates" the feeling of drowning. This is not the case. You feel that you are drowning because you *are* drowning—or, rather, being drowned, albeit slowly and under controlled conditions. . . . I waited for a while until I abruptly felt a slow cascade of water going up my nose. . . . The inhalation brought the damp cloths tight against my nostrils, as if a huge, wet paw had been suddenly and annihilatingly clamped over my face. Unable to determine whether I was breathing in or out, and flooded more with sheer panic than with mere water, I triggered the pre-arranged signal and felt the unbelievable relief of being pulled upright and having the soaking and stifling layers pulled off me.

Christopher Hitchens,
"Believe Me, It's Torture," Vanity Fair, *August 2008.*
www.vanityfair.com.

Judge Advocate General of the Navy, who says, "Waterboarding was devised in the Spanish Inquisition. Next to the rack and thumbscrews, it's the most iconic example of torture." Are we to really believe that these men are not only radical pacifists but should have never been put in "charge of decisions on war and peace"?

No offense to Mr. Thiessen's experience as a speechwriter for the former secretary of defense, but I would prefer to trust the judgment of these men—these radical pacifists—who are intimately familiar with torture, war, and the best means of keeping our nation safe.

A Different Perspective on Interrogation

The rest of Thiessen's argument is like a matryoshka doll [or a Russian nesting doll] of false choices. Embedded in his *ad hominem* false dichotomy (you either accept torture or you're a radical pacifist) is a false dichotomy between accepting waterboarding and resignation to another terrorist attack.

Contrary to Thiessen's assertion, the evidence that waterboarding helped stop a number of terrorist attacks is debatable. While you will find many former members of the [George W.] Bush administration (e.g., [former vice president] Dick Cheney, Mr. Thiessen) making absolutist claims about its efficacy, those who actually know the most about the subject (i.e., the military, CIA, FBI officials) are generally more skeptical. And for good reason: The claims about the effectiveness of torture have been debated—and proven inconclusive—throughout history.

Fortunately, waterboarding and other "enhanced interrogation techniques" are not the only means of extracting information from our enemies. In fact, the most successful interrogation of an al Qaeda operative by U.S. officials after 9/11 [September 11, 2001, terrorist attacks on the United States] involved a less dramatic interrogation tool: sugar cookies.[1] Even the fact that Khalid Sheikh Mohammed was subjected to waterboarding 183 times in a one-month period casts doubts on its utility and shows that it would be completely worthless in the hypothetical "ticking time bomb" scenarios that torture-apologists tend to favor. Perhaps Thiessen should familiarize himself with the fallacy of exhaustive hypotheses before making such overly broad, and spurious, claims about what is required to prevent future terrorist attacks.

Even weaker than the logic of the argument is the moral justification. Perhaps torture would make sense in a pagan society where the nation-state is of primary importance and all

1. Al Qaeda operative Abu Jandal provided authorities with information after they brought him sugar-free cookies that he could eat despite his diabetes.

actions are ultimately justifiable if they serve nationalist ends. But in a nation whose ethical foundation is rooted in a Judeo-Christian concept of justice, torture by state agents should always be considered impermissible. The reason that there is a long history of just warfare theory but no corresponding "just torture theory" is because torture is inherently antithetical to justice and morality.

As Russell Saltzman [associate editor of *First Things*] wrote back in April [2009],

> [T]orture is wrong because it can never serve a moral purpose. It serves instead only an immoral purpose: the destruction of an individual's personhood. It is violence against the imago Dei, the image of God carried by every person.
>
> Crucial to the use of torture is the intentional, systematic, step-by-step reduction of identity and selfhood, the purposeful diminution of the person as person, as the image of God cheapened to something less, to something "unperson." The "other" is depersonalized. It is this process of thinking which gives us license for abortion, euthanasia, capital punishment, and torture—everything that strips the person of personal humanity.

Pagan Values

Despite the weakness of Thiessen's argument, his position is worthy of discussion. After all, *First Things* is dedicated to "religiously informed public philosophy" so a position based on religious—specifically pagan—values is deserving of respectful treatment. But the fact that Thiessen feels comfortable making an argument based on pagan ethics in a journal [*National Review Online*] with a long heritage of Christian (and specifically Catholic) influence is a sign of how far we have come in the debasement of conservatism.

Of course, pagans—and Christians who accept pagan ideals when convenient—have always been with us and they deserve their place in the public square. But the global war on terror has allowed them to dominate certain conversations, leading us away from conservative policy proposals that are rooted in Christian principles. Rather than push back, we Christians have remained silent and treated an issue once considered unthinkable—the acceptability of torture—as if it's a practice that must be accepted under the banner of "realism." Perhaps we should not be surprised then to find the tables turned on us and the idea that *opposition to torture* is barely worthy of respect.

But Christians should be unequivocal in our opposition: Torture is immoral and should be clearly and forcefully denounced. We continue to shame ourselves and our Creator by refusing to speak out against such outrages to human dignity. If that means that we will be slandered as radical pacifists, then we should wear the label proudly.

[Author's] note: As a commenter pointed out, my use of the term "pagan" can be confusing. The term is broad but I intended it in a more narrow sense. Essentially, I meant it to refer to the types of societies and thinkers that [journalist] Robert Kaplan refers to in *Warrior Politics: Why Leadership Demands a Pagan Ethos*: The ancient Greeks and Romans, the Asian warrior-cultures (such as those that produced thinkers like Sun Tzu), the pre-UN [United Nations] secular Europeans (such as [Niccolò] Machiavelli). The virtues of these types of pagans are the ones that Kaplan et al. want to replace Judeo-Christian morality.

Waterboarding Is Torture

Addendum: Invariably, such a discussion will lead someone to claim that "waterboarding is not torture." While I can respect those who wish to claim that there are times when torture is necessary, I have no patience for those who play semantic Orwellian games [that undermine a free society]. Waterboarding has always been considered a technique of torture. The U.S.

government considered waterboarding to be torture when it was used on our soldiers in World War II—and it would be considered torture if used on our servicemembers today.

For those still unclear on the concept, the legal definition of torture to which the U.S. subscribes can be found in the UN Convention Against Torture [and Other Cruel, Inhuman or Degrading Treatment or Punishment]:

> For the purposes of this Convention, torture means any act by which severe pain or suffering, whether physical or mental, is intentionally inflicted on a person for such purposes as obtaining from him or a third person information or a confession, punishing him for an act he or a third person has committed or is suspected of having committed, or intimidating or coercing him or a third person, or for any reason based on discrimination of any kind, when such pain or suffering is inflicted by or at the instigation of or with the consent or acquiescence of a public official or other person acting in an official capacity. It does not include pain or suffering rising only from, inherent in or incidental to lawful sanctions.

VIEWPOINT 5

"If we are willing to act in a way that guarantees the misery and death of some considerable number of innocent children, why spare the rod with known terrorists?"

If a Nation Is Willing to Wage War, It Should Be Willing to Condone Torture

Sam Harris

Sam Harris is a neuroscientist and the author of The End of Faith: Religion, Terror, and the Future of Reason. *In the following viewpoint, he argues that if modern war is sometimes necessary and ethically allowable, then torture should be as well. He notes that collateral damage in warfare kills innocent women and children, and he suggests that torture applied to known terrorists like Osama bin Laden would be relatively justified. He concludes that even if torture is not reliable, the chance that it might provide useful information might justify it in certain rare circumstances.*

Sam Harris, "In Defense of Torture," *Huffington Post*, October 17, 2005.

As you read, consider the following questions:

1. Why does Harris say that Abu Ghraib may be one of the costliest foreign policy blunders of the last century?
2. What does Harris believe would happen if all the good people on earth adopted Gandhi's ethics?
3. What does Harris imagine a torture pill might do, and does he believe that such a pill would be ethically superior to other methods of torture?

Imagine that a known terrorist has planted a bomb in the heart of a nearby city. He now sits in your custody. Rather than conceal his guilt, he gloats about the forthcoming explosion and the magnitude of human suffering it will cause. Given this state of affairs—in particular, given that there is still time to prevent an imminent atrocity—it seems that subjecting this unpleasant fellow to torture may be justifiable. For those who make it their business to debate the ethics of torture this is known as the "ticking-bomb" case.

Torture in Rare Circumstances

While the most realistic version of the ticking-bomb case may not persuade everyone that torture is ethically acceptable, adding further embellishments seems to awaken the Grand Inquisitor in most of us. If a conventional explosion doesn't move you, consider a nuclear bomb hidden in midtown Manhattan. If bombs seem too impersonal an evil, picture your seven-year-old daughter being slowly asphyxiated in a warehouse just five minutes away, while the man in your custody holds the keys to her release. If your daughter won't tip the scales, then add the daughters of every couple for a thousand miles—millions of little girls have, by some perverse negligence on the part of our government, come under the control of an evil genius who now sits before you in shackles. Clearly, the consequences of one person's uncooperativeness can be made so grave, and his malevolence and culpability so transparent, as to stir even a self-hating moral relativist from his dogmatic slumbers.

I am one of the few people I know of who has argued in print that torture may be an ethical necessity in our war on terror. In the aftermath of Abu Ghraib [an American prison in Iraq where guards tortured prisoners], this is not a comfortable position to have publicly adopted. There is no question that Abu Ghraib was a travesty, and there is no question that it has done our country lasting harm. Indeed, the Abu Ghraib scandal may be one of the costliest foreign policy blunders to occur in the last century, given the degree to which it simultaneously inflamed the Muslim world and eroded the sympathies of our democratic allies. While we hold the moral high ground in our war on terror, we appear to hold it less and less. Our casual abuse of ordinary prisoners is largely responsible for this. Documented abuses at Abu Ghraib, Guantánamo Bay [an American prison in Cuba for those accused of terrorism] and elsewhere have now inspired legislation prohibiting "cruel, inhuman or degrading" treatment of military prisoners. And yet, these developments do not shed much light on the ethics of torturing people like Osama bin Laden [a terrorist linked to the September 11, 2001, attacks on the United States] when we get them in custody.

I will now present an argument for the use of torture in rare circumstances. While many people have objected, on emotional grounds, to my defense of torture, no one has pointed out a flaw in my argument. I hope my case for torture is wrong, as I would be much happier standing side by side with all the good people who oppose torture categorically. I invite any reader who discovers a problem with my argument to point it out to me in the comment section of this blog. I would be sincerely grateful to have my mind changed on this subject.

Torture Is No Worse than War

Most readers will undoubtedly feel at this point that torture is evil and that we are wise not to practice it. Even if we can't quite muster a retort to the ticking-bomb case, most of us take refuge in the fact that the paradigmatic case will almost never arise. It seems, however, that this position is impossible to square with our willingness to wage modern war in the first place.

In modern warfare, "collateral damage"—the maiming and killing innocent noncombatants—is unavoidable. And it will remain unavoidable for the foreseeable future. Collateral damage would be a problem even if our bombs were far "smarter" than they are now. It would also be a problem even if we resolved to fight only defensive wars. There is no escaping the fact that whenever we drop bombs, we drop them with the knowledge that some number of children will be blinded, disemboweled, paralyzed, orphaned, and killed by them.

The only way to rule out collateral damage would be to refuse to fight wars under any circumstances. As a foreign policy, this would leave us with something like the absolute pacifism of [Indian revolutionary Mahatma] Gandhi. While pacifism in this form can constitute a direct confrontation with injustice (and requires considerable bravery), it is only applicable to a limited range of human conflicts. Where it is not applicable, it is seems flagrantly immoral. We would do well to reflect on Gandhi's remedy for the Holocaust: He believed that the Jews should have committed mass suicide, because this "would have aroused the world and the people of Germany to [dictator Adolf] Hitler's violence." We might wonder what a world full of pacifists would have done once it had grown "aroused"—commit suicide as well? There seems no question that if all the good people in the world adopted Gandhi's ethics, the thugs would inherit the earth.

So we can now ask, if we are willing to act in a way that guarantees the misery and death of some considerable number of innocent children, why spare the rod with known terrorists? I find it genuinely bizarre that while the torture of Osama bin Laden himself could be expected to provoke convulsions of conscience among our leaders, the perfectly foreseeable (and therefore accepted) slaughter of children does not. What is the difference between pursuing a course of action where we run the risk of inadvertently subjecting some innocent men to torture, and pursuing one in which we will inadvertently kill far greater numbers of innocent men, women, and children? Rather, it seems obvious that the misapplication of torture should be far *less* troubling to us than collateral damage: there are, after all, no *infants* interned at Guantánamo Bay. Torture need not even impose a significant risk of death or permanent injury on its victims; while the collaterally damaged are, almost by definition, crippled or killed. The ethical divide that seems to be opening up here suggests that those who are willing to drop bombs might want to abduct the nearest and dearest of suspected terrorists—their wives, mothers, and daughters—and torture *them* as well, assuming anything profitable to our side might come of it. Admittedly, this would be a ghastly result to have reached by logical argument, and we will want to find some way of escaping it. But there seems no question that accidentally torturing an innocent man is better than accidentally blowing him and his children to bits.

Feelings About Violence Should Not Influence Ethics

In this context, we should note that many variables influence our feelings about an act of physical violence. The philosopher Jonathan Glover points out that "in modern war, what is most shocking is a poor guide to what is most harmful." To learn that one's grandfather flew a bombing mission over Dresden [Germany] in the Second World War is one thing; to hear that he killed five little girls and their mother with a

No Categorical Argument Against Torture

I am not alone in thinking that there are potential circumstances in which the use of torture would be ethically justifiable. Liberal Senator Charles Schumer has publicly stated that most U.S. senators would support torture to find out the location of a ticking time bomb. Such "ticking-bomb" scenarios have been widely criticized as unrealistic. But realism is not the point of such thought experiments. The point is that unless you have an argument that rules out torture in idealized cases, you don't have a categorical argument against the use of torture. As nuclear and biological terrorism become increasingly possible, it is in everyone's interest for men and women of goodwill to determine what should be done if a prisoner appears to have operational knowledge of an imminent atrocity (and may even claim to possess such knowledge), but won't otherwise talk about it.

Sam Harris,
"Response to Controversy: Version 1.8,"
August 11, 2009. www.samharris.org.

shovel is another. We can be sure that he would have killed many more women and girls by dropping bombs from pristine heights, and they are likely to have died equally horrible deaths, but his culpability would not appear the same. There is much to be said about the disparity here, but the relevance to the ethics of torture should be obvious. If you think that the equivalence between torture and collateral damage does not hold, because torture is up close and personal while stray bombs aren't, you stand convicted of a failure of imagination on at least two counts: First, a moment's reflection on the horrors that must have been visited upon innocent Afghanis and Iraqis by our bombs will reveal that they are on par with those of any dungeon. If our intuition about the wrongness of torture is born of an aversion to how people generally behave while being tortured, we should note that this particular infelicity could be circumvented pharmacologically, because paralytic drugs make it unnecessary for screaming ever to be heard or writhing seen. We could easily devise methods of torture that would render a torturer as blind to the plight of his victims as a bomber pilot is at thirty thousand feet. Consequently, our natural aversion to the sights and sounds of the dungeon provide no foothold for those who would argue against the use of torture.

To demonstrate just how abstract the torments of the tortured can be made to seem, we need only imagine an ideal "torture pill"—a drug that would deliver both the instruments of torture and the instrument of their concealment. The action of the pill would be to produce transitory paralysis and transitory misery of a kind that no human being would willingly submit to a second time. Imagine how we torturers would feel if, after giving this pill to captive terrorists, each lay down for what appeared to be an hour's nap only to arise and immediately confess everything he knows about the workings of his organization. Might we not be tempted to call it a "truth pill" in the end? No, there is no ethical difference to be found in how the suffering of the tortured or the collaterally damaged appears.

Unreliable Confessions Are Not an Argument Against Torture

Opponents of torture will be quick to argue that confessions elicited by torture are notoriously unreliable. Given the foregoing, however, this objection seems to lack its usual force. Make these confessions as unreliable as you like—the chance that our interests will be advanced in any instance of torture need only equal the chance of such occasioned by the dropping of a single bomb. What was the chance that the dropping of bomb number 117 on Kandahar [Afghanistan] would affect the demise of al Qaeda? It had to be pretty slim. Enter Khalid Sheikh Mohammed: our most valuable capture in our war on terror. Here is a character who actually seems to have stepped out of a philosopher's thought experiment. U.S. officials now believe that his was the hand that decapitated the *Wall Street Journal* reporter Daniel Pearl [in 2002]. Whether or not this is true, his membership in al Qaeda more or less rules out his "innocence" in any important sense, and his rank in the organization suggests that his knowledge of planned atrocities must be extensive. The bomb has been ticking ever since September 11th, 2001. Given the damage we were willing to cause to the bodies and minds of innocent children in Afghanistan and Iraq, our disavowal of torture in the case of Khalid Sheikh Mohammed seems perverse. If there is even one chance in a million that he will tell us something under torture that will lead to the further dismantling of al Qaeda, it seems that we should use every means at our disposal to get him talking. (In fact, the *New York Times* has reported that Khalid Sheikh Mohammed was tortured in a procedure known as "waterboarding [a technique of controlled drowning]," despite our official disavowal of this practice.)

Which way should the balance swing? Assuming that we want to maintain a coherent ethical position on these matters, this appears to be a circumstance of forced choice: If we are willing to drop bombs, or even risk that rifle rounds might go astray, we should be willing to torture a certain class of criminal suspects and military prisoners; if we are unwilling to torture, we should be unwilling to wage modern war.

Viewpoint 6

> "Nonviolent action ... is the most powerful political tool available to challenge oppression."

Nonviolence Is a Force for Social Change

Stephen Zunes

Stephen Zunes is a professor of Politics and International Studies at the University of San Francisco. In the following viewpoint, he argues that nonviolent resistance is more effective at ending oppression than violent resistance. He points to research that suggests that nonviolent resistance has a greater likelihood of success in overthrowing oppressive regimes. Further, he argues that nonviolent movements are more likely to establish democratic governments, rather than replacing one repressive regime with another. He concludes that more and more resistance movements are recognizing the power of nonviolent action.

As you read, consider the following questions:

1. According to Freedom House, what fraction of countries that made the transition from dictatorship did so through nonviolent means?

Stephen Zunes, "Weapons of Mass Democracy," *Yes! Magazine*, September 16, 2009.

2. According to Zunes, why are pro-government elements more willing to compromise with nonviolent insurgents?
3. Why does Zunes argue that there is no standardized formula for success in nonviolent movements that a foreign government could put together?

On the outskirts of a desert town in the Moroccan-occupied territory of Western Sahara, about a dozen young activists are gathered. They are involved in their country's long struggle for freedom. A group of foreigners—veterans of protracted resistance movements—is conducting a training session in the optimal use of a "weapons system" that is increasingly deployed in struggles for freedom around the world. The workshop leaders pass out Arabic translations of writings on the theory and dynamics of revolutionary struggle and lead the participants in a series of exercises designed to enhance their strategic and tactical thinking.

Unarmed Insurrection

These trainers are not veterans of guerrilla warfare, however, but of unarmed insurrections against repressive regimes. The materials they hand out are not the words of Che Guevara [a fighter in the Cuban revolution], but of Gene Sharp, the former Harvard scholar who has pioneered the study of strategic nonviolent action. And the weapons they advocate employing are not guns and bombs, but strikes, boycotts, mass demonstrations, tax refusal, alternative media, and refusal to obey official orders.

Serbs, South Africans, Filipinos, Georgians, and other veterans of successful nonviolent struggles are sharing their knowledge and experience with those still fighting dictators and occupation armies.

The young Western Saharans know how an armed struggle by an older generation of their countrymen failed to dislodge the Moroccans, who first invaded their country back in 1975.

They have seen how Morocco's allies on the UN [United Nations] Security Council—led by France and the United States—blocked enforcement of UN resolutions supporting their right to self-determination. With the failure of both armed struggle and diplomacy to bring them freedom, they have decided to instead employ a force more powerful.

The Rise of Nonviolence

The long-standing assumption that dictatorial regimes can only be overthrown through armed struggle or foreign military intervention is coming under increasing challenge. Though nonviolent action has a long and impressive history going back centuries, events in recent decades have demonstrated more than ever that nonviolent action is not just a form of principled witness utilized by religious pacifists. It is the most powerful political tool available to challenge oppression.

It was not the leftist guerrillas of the New People's Army [that] brought down the U.S.-backed [Ferdinand] Marcos dictatorship in the Philippines. It was nuns praying the rosary in front of the regime's tanks, and the millions of others who brought greater Manila to a standstill.

It was not the 11 weeks of bombing that brought down Serbian leader Slobodan Milosevic, the infamous "butcher of the Balkans." It was a nonviolent resistance movement led by young students, whose generation had been sacrificed in a series of bloody military campaigns against neighboring Yugoslav republics, and who were able to mobilize a large cross-section of the population to rise up against a stolen election.

It was not the armed wing of the African National Congress that brought majority rule to South Africa. It was workers, students, and township dwellers who—through the use of strikes, boycotts, the creation of alternative institutions, and other acts of defiance—made it impossible for the apartheid system to continue.

It was not NATO [the North Atlantic Treaty Organization] that brought down the Communist regimes of Eastern Europe or freed the Baltic republics from Soviet control. It was Polish dock workers, East German church people, Estonian folk singers, Czech intellectuals, and millions of ordinary citizens.

Similarly, such tyrants as Jean-Claude Duvalier in Haiti, Moussa Traoré in Mali, King Gyanendra in Nepal, General Suharto in Indonesia, and, most recently, Maumoon Gayoom in the Maldives were forced to cede power when it became clear that they were powerless in the face of massive nonviolent resistance and noncooperation.

The power of nonviolent action has been acknowledged even by such groups as Freedom House, a Washington [D.C.]-based organization with close ties to the foreign policy establishment. Its 2005 study observed that, of the nearly 70 countries that have made the transition from dictatorship to varying degrees of democracy in the past 30 years, only a small minority did so through armed struggle from below or reform instigated from above. Hardly any new democracies resulted from foreign invasion. In nearly three-quarters of the transitions, change was rooted in democratic civil society organizations that employed nonviolent methods. In addition, the study noted that countries where nonviolent civil resistance movements played a major role tend to have freer and more stable democratic systems.

A different study, published last year [2008] in the journal *International Security*, used an expanded database and analyzed 323 major insurrections in support of self-determination and democratic rule since 1900. It found that violent resistance was successful only 26 percent of the time, whereas nonviolent campaigns had a 53 percent success rate.

From the poorest nations of Africa to the relatively affluent countries of Eastern Europe; from Communist regimes to right-wing military dictatorships; from across the cultural, geographic and ideological spectrum, democratic and progressive forces have recognized the power of nonviolent action to free them from oppression. This has not come, in most cases, from a moral or spiritual commitment to nonviolence, but simply because it works.

Why Nonviolent Action Works

Armed resistance, even for a just cause, can terrify people not yet committed to the struggle, making it easier for a government to justify violent repression and use of military force in the name of protecting the population. Even rioting and vandalism can turn public opinion against a movement, which is why some governments have employed agent provocateurs to encourage such violence. The use of force against unarmed resistance movements, on the other hand, usually creates greater sympathy for the government's opponents. As with the martial art of aikido, nonviolent opposition movements can engage the force of the state's repression and use it to effectively disarm the force directed against them.

In addition, unarmed campaigns involve a range of participants far beyond the young able-bodied men normally found in the ranks of armed guerrillas. As the movement grows in strength, it can include a large cross-section of the population. Though most repressive governments are well-prepared to deal with a violent insurgency, they tend to be less prepared to counter massive non-cooperation by old, middle aged, and young. When millions of people defy official orders by engaging in illegal demonstrations, going out on strike, violating curfews, refusing to pay taxes, and otherwise refusing to recognize the legitimacy of the state, the state no longer has power. During the "people power" uprising against the Marcos dictatorship in the Philippines, for example, Marcos lost power not through the defeat of his troops and the storming of the Malacañang Palace but when—due to massive defiance of his orders—the palace became the only part of the country he still effectively controlled.

Gene Sharp and Nonviolence

Gene Sharp, a retired Harvard researcher, is considered the godfather of nonviolent resistance. Since the early 1970s, his work has served as the template for taking on authoritarian regimes from Burma [officially the Republic of the Union of Myanmar] to Belgrade. A list of his 198 methods for nonviolent action . . . has been translated . . . into two dozen languages ranging from Azeri to Vietnamese.

Scott Peterson, "Iran Protestors: The Harvard Professor Behind Their Tactics," Christian Science Monitor, *December 29, 2009. www.csmonitor.com.*

Furthermore, pro-government elements tend to be more willing to compromise with nonviolent insurgents, who are less likely to physically harm their opponents when they take power. When massive demonstrations challenged the military junta in Chile in the late 1980s, military leaders convinced the dictator Augusto Pinochet to agree to the nonviolent protesters' demands for a referendum on his continued rule and to accept the results when the vote went against him.

Unarmed movements also increase the likelihood of defections and non-cooperation by police and military personnel, who will generally fight in self-defense against armed guerrillas but are hesitant to shoot into unarmed crowds. Such defiance was key to the downfall of dictatorships in East Germany, Mali, Serbia, the Philippines, Ukraine, and elsewhere. The moral power of nonviolence is crucial to the ability of an opposition movement to reframe the perceptions of the public, political elites, and the military.

A Democratizing Force

In many cases, armed revolutionaries—trained in martial values, the power of the gun, and a leadership model based upon a secret, elite vanguard—have themselves become authoritarian rulers once in power. In addition, because civil war often leads to serious economic, environmental, and social problems, the new leadership is tempted to embrace emergency powers they are later reluctant to surrender. Algeria and Guinea-Bissau experienced military coups soon after their successful armed independence struggles, while victorious Communist guerrillas in a number of countries simply established new dictatorships.

By contrast, successful nonviolent movements build broad coalitions based on compromise and consensus. The new order that emerges from that foundation tends to be pluralistic and democratic.

Liberal democracy carries no guarantee of social justice, but many of those involved in pro-democracy struggles have latter played a key role in leading the effort to establish more equitable social and economic orders. For example, the largely nonviolent indigenous peasant and worker movements that ended a series of military dictatorships in Bolivia in the 1980s formed the basis of the movement that brought Evo Morales and his allies to power, resulting in a series of exciting reforms benefiting the country's poor, indigenous majority.

Another reason nonviolent movements tend to create sustainable democracy is that, in the course of the movement, alternative institutions are created that empower ordinary people. For example, autonomous workers' councils eroded the authority of party apparatchiks in Polish industry even as the Communist Party still nominally ruled the country. In South Africa, popularly elected local governments and people's courts in the black townships completely usurped the authority of administrators and judges appointed by the apartheid [segregation] regime long before majority rule came to the country as a whole.

Recent successes of nonviolent tactics have raised concerns about their use by those with undemocratic aims. However, it is virtually impossible for an undemocratic result to emerge from a movement based upon broad popular support. Local elites, often with the support of foreign powers, have historically promoted regime change through military invasions, coup d'états, and other kinds of violent seizures of power that install an undemocratic minority. Nonviolent "people power" movements, by contrast, make peaceful regime change possible by empowering pro-democratic majorities.

Indeed, every successful nonviolent insurrection has been a homegrown movement rooted in the realization by the masses that their rulers were illegitimate and that the political system would not redress injustice. By contrast, a nonviolent insurrection is unlikely to succeed when the movement's leadership and agenda do not have the backing of the majority of the population. This is why the 2002–2003 "strike" by some privileged sectors of Venezuela's oil industry failed to bring down the democratically elected government of Hugo Chávez, while the widely supported strikes in the Iranian oil fields against the Shah in 1978–1979 were key in bringing down his autocratic regime.

Homegrown Movements Alone Can Inspire a Majority

Unlike most successful unarmed insurrections, Iran slid back under autocratic rule after the overthrow of the Shah. Now [2009], hard-line clerics and their allies have themselves been challenged by a nonviolent pro-democracy movement. Like most governments facing popular challenges, rather than acknowledging their own failures, the Iranian regime has sought to blame outsiders for fomenting the resistance. Given the sordid history of U.S. interventionism in that country—including the overthrow of Iran's last democratic government in 1953 in a CIA-backed military coup—some are taking those claims seriously. However, Iranians have engaged in nonviolent action for generations, not just in opposition to the Shah, but going back to the 1890–1892 boycotts against concessions to the British and the 1905–1908 Constitutional Revolution. There is little Americans can teach Iranians about such civil resistance.

Citing funding from Western governments and foundations, similar charges of powerful Western interests being responsible for nonviolent insurrections have also been made in regard to recent successful pro-democracy movements in Serbia, Georgia, and Ukraine.

However, while outside funding can be useful in enabling opposition groups to buy computers, print literature, and promote their work, it cannot cause a nonviolent liberal democratic revolution to take place any more than Soviet financial and material support for leftist movements in previous decades could cause an armed socialist revolution to take place.

Successful revolutions, whatever their ideological orientation, are the result of certain social conditions. Indeed, no amount of money could force hundreds of thousands of people to leave their jobs, homes, schools, and families to face down heavily armed police and tanks and put their bodies on the line. They must be motivated by a desire for change so strong they are willing to make the sacrifices and take the personal risks to bring it about.

In any case, there is no standardized formula for success that a foreign government could put together, since the history, culture, and political alignments of each country are unique. No foreign government can recruit or mobilize the large numbers of ordinary civilians necessary to build a movement capable of effectively challenging the established political leadership, much less of toppling a government.

Even workshops like the one for the Western Saharan activists, usually funded through nonprofit, nongovernmental [organization (NGO)] foundations, generally focus on providing generic information on the theory, dynamics, and history of nonviolent action. There is broad consensus among workshop leaders that only those involved in the struggles themselves are in a position to make tactical and strategic decisions, so they tend not to give specific advice. However, such capacity-building efforts—like comparable NGO projects for sustainable development, human rights, equality for women and minorities, economic justice, and the environment—can be an effective means of fostering international solidarity.

Nonviolence Is a Worldwide Force

Back in Western Sahara, anti-occupation activists, building on their own experiences against the Moroccan occupation and on what they learned from the workshop, press on in the struggle for their country's freedom. In the face of severe repression from U.S.-backed Moroccan forces, the movement continues with demonstrations, leafleting, graffiti-writing, flag-waving, boycotts, and other actions. One prominent leader of the movement, Aminatou Haidar, won the Robert F. Kennedy Human Rights Award last November [2008], and she has been twice nominated for the Nobel Peace Prize.

Those in the Western Sahara resistance are among the growing numbers of people around the world struggling against repression who have recognized that armed resistance is more likely to magnify their suffering than relieve it.

From Western Sahara to West Papua [occupied by Indonesia] to the West Bank [a territory occupied by Israel], people are engaged in nonviolent resistance against foreign occupation. Similarly, from Egypt to Iran to Burma [officially the Republic of the Union of Myanmar], people are fighting nonviolently for freedom from dictatorial rule.

Recent history has shown that power ultimately resides in the people, not in the state; that nonviolent strategies can be more powerful than guns; and that nonviolent action is a form of conflict that can build, rather than destroy.

VIEWPOINT 7

"Pretending that all violence is the same is very convenient for supposedly anti-violence privileged people who benefit from the violence of the state and have much to lose from the violence of revolution."

Nonviolence Is Ineffective at Bringing About Social Change

Peter Gelderloos

Peter Gelderloos is a radical community organizer from Virginia. In the following viewpoint, he argues that pacifism is not revolutionary. He says that those who advocate violent revolution are intelligent, realistic, effective, and risk more than those who advocate nonviolence. He says that pacifists are able to renounce violence because they are privileged and do not have a real experience of oppression. He argues that tactical violence in the name of revolution is morally different than the constant violence perpetuated by the state.

Peter Gelderloos, "Chapter 6: Nonviolence Is Deluded," *How Nonviolence Protects the State*. South End Press, pp. 118-123, 2007.

As you read, consider the following questions:

1. According to Gelderloos, what did a government commission find about the typical rioter following the Detroit riots of 1967?
2. Which conflict does Gelderloos say makes up a large part of the textbooks used by the United States in counterinsurgency warfare?
3. Who was Leon Czolgosz, according to the author?

Often, pacifists prefer to characterize themselves as righteous than to logically defend their position. Most people who have heard the arguments of nonviolence have witnessed the formulation or assumption that nonviolence is the path of the dedicated and disciplined, and that violence is the "easy way out," a giving in to base emotions. This is patently absurd. Nonviolence is the easy way out. People who choose to commit themselves to nonviolence face a far more comfortable future than those who choose to commit themselves to revolution. A prisoner of the black liberation movement told me in correspondence that when he joined the struggle (as a teenager, no less), he knew he would end up either dead or in prison. Many of his comrades are dead. For continuing the struggle behind prison walls, he has been locked up in solitary confinement for longer than I have been alive. Compare this with the recent comfortable, commemorated deaths of David Dellinger and Phil Berrigan [both pacifist activists]. Nonviolent activists can give their lives to their cause, and a few have, but, unlike militant activists, they do not face a point of no return after which there is no going back to a comfortable life. They can always save themselves by compromising their total opposition, and most do.

Activism Is Not Anger

Aside from reflecting an ignorance of the reality of the different consequences of certain political actions, the belief that non-pacifist struggle is the easy way out is often tinged with racism. The authors [Gordon Faison and Bob Irwin] of the essay "Why Nonviolence?" do their best throughout the entire essay to avoid mention of race, but in the question-and-answer section they provide a veiled response to criticisms that pacifism is racist by painting "oppressed people" (black people) as angry and impulse-driven. "Q: Demanding nonviolent behavior from oppressed people toward their oppressors is senseless and unfair! They need to act out their anger!" The authors' "answer" to this contrived criticism of nonviolence includes many of the typical and deluded fallacies: the authors counsel people who are far more oppressed than they are to have patience with conditions they couldn't possibly comprehend; the authors advise people of color to act in a way that is "ennobling and pragmatic"; the authors forestall criticisms of racism by dropping the name of a token person of color; and the authors conclude by tacitly threatening that militant activism on the part of people of color will result in abandonment and betrayal by powerful white "allies." To wit:

> As for unfairness, if the oppressed could wish it away, they would no longer be oppressed. There is no pain-free road to liberation. Given the inevitability of suffering, it is both ennobling and pragmatic to present nonviolent discipline and suffering (as did Martin Luther King Jr.) as imperatives. "Acting out anger" in a way that costs a group allies is a luxury serious movements cannot afford.

Knowledge Leads Revolutionaries

Pacifists delude themselves in thinking of revolutionary activism as being impulsive, irrational, and coming solely from "anger." In fact, revolutionary activism, in some of its manifestations, has a pronounced intellectual streak. After the Detroit riots of 1967, a *government* commission found that the typical rioter (in addition to being proud of his or her race and hostile to white people and middle-class black people) "is substantially better informed about politics than Negroes who were not involved in the riots." George Jackson [a member of the African American revolutionary Black Panther Party] educated himself in prison, and emphasized in his writings the need for militant black people to study their historical relationship to their oppressors and learn the "scientific principles" of urban guerrilla warfare. The [Black] Panthers read Mao, Kwame Nkrumah, and Frantz Fanon,[1] and required new members to educate themselves on the political theories behind their revolution. When he was finally captured and brought to trial, revolutionary New Afrikan anarchist Kuwasi Balagoon [who was also a Black Panther] rejected the court's legitimacy and proclaimed the right of black people to liberate themselves in a statement many pacifists could learn volumes from:

> Before becoming a clandestine revolutionary I was a tenant organizer and was arrested for menacing a 270-pound colonial building superintendent with a machete, who physically stopped the delivery of oil to a building I didn't live in, but had helped to organize. Being an organizer for the Community Council on Housing I took part in not only organizing rent strikes, but pressed slumlords to make repairs and maintain heat and hot water, killed rats, represented tenants in court, stopped illegal evictions, faced off city marshals, helped turn rents into repair resources and collective ownership by tenants and demonstrated whenever the needs of tenants were at stake.... Then I began to realize that with all this effort, we couldn't put a dent in the problem...
>
> Legal rituals have no effect on the historic process of armed struggle by oppressed nations. The war will continue and intensify, and as for me, I'd rather be in jail or in the grave than do anything other than fight the oppressor of my people. The New Afrikan Nation [a proposed African American majority nation in the southeastern United States] as

1. Mao Zedong led a violent revolution in China; Kwame Nkrumah was a 20th-century leader of Ghana; Frantz Fanon was a philosopher and revolutionary.

> well as the Native American nations are colonialized within the present confines of the United States, as the Puerto Rican and Mexicano nations are colonialized within as well as outside the present confines of the United States. We have a right to resist, to expropriate money and arms, to kill the enemy of our people, to bomb and do whatever else aids us in winning, and we will win.

Nonviolence Is Simplistic

In comparison, the strategic and tactical analysis of nonviolent activism is rather simplistic, rarely rising above the regurgitation of hackneyed clichés and moralistic truisms. The amount of studious preparations required to successfully carry out militant actions, compared with the amount required for nonviolent actions, also contradicts the perception that revolutionary activism is impulsive.

People willing to acknowledge the violence of revolution—it is misleading to talk about choosing violence because violence is inherent in social revolution and the oppressive status quo that precedes it, whether we use violent means or not—are more likely to understand the sacrifices involved. Any knowledge of what revolutionaries prepare themselves for and go through demonstrates the cruelly ignorant farce of the pacifist proclamation that revolutionary violence is impulsive. As already mentioned, the writings of Frantz Fanon were among the most influential for black revolutionaries in the United States during the black liberation movement. The last chapter of his book *The Wretched of the Earth* deals entirely with "colonial war and mental disorders," with the psychological trauma incurred as a matter of course from colonialism and the "total war" waged by the French against the Algerian freedom fighters [during the 1950s and 1960s] (a war, I should note, that makes up a large part of the textbook used by the US in counterinsurgency warfare and wars of occupation up to the present moment). People who fight for revolution do know what they are getting into, to the extent that the horror of these things can be known. But do pacifists?

A further delusion (expressed by pacifists who want to appear militant and powerful) is that pacifists do fight back, only nonviolently. This is rubbish. Sitting down and locking arms is not fighting, it is a recalcitrant capitulation. In a situation involving a bully or a centralized power apparatus, physically fighting back discourages future attacks because it raises the costs of oppression incurred by the oppressor. The meek resistance of nonviolence only makes it easier for the attacks to continue. At the next protest, for instance, see how reluctant the police are to fence in militant groups such as the black bloc[2] and subject them all to mass arrest. The cops know that they'll need one or two cops for every protestor and that some of them are going to end up badly hurt. The peaceful, on the other hand, can be barricaded in by a relatively small number of cops, who can then go into the crowd at their leisure and carry off the limp protestors one by one.

Palestine is another example. There can be no doubt that the Palestinians are an inconvenience to the Israeli state, and that the Israeli state has no concern for the well-being of the Palestinians. If the Palestinians hadn't made the Israeli occupation and every successive aggression so costly, all the Palestinian land would be seized, except for a few reservations to hold the necessary number of surplus laborers to supplement the Israeli economy, and the Palestinians would be a distant memory in a long line of extinct peoples. Palestinian resistance, including suicide bombings, has helped ensure Palestinian survival against a far more powerful enemy.

Nonviolence Is Not Revolutionary

Nonviolence further deludes itself and its converts with the truism "Society has always been violent. It is nonviolence that is revolutionary." In practice, our society honors and com-

2. The black bloc is a protest tactic in which protestors wear black, cover their faces, and often carry truncheons.

memorates both pro-state violence and respectable, dissident pacifism. The very activist who claimed that our society is already pro-violence can drop the name of Leon Czolgosz (the anarchist who assassinated President [William] McKinley [in 1901]) in a guest op-ed in the local corporate newspaper and know that a mainstream audience will respond to that violent personage with condemnation. Meanwhile, the same activist references pacifists like King and [Indian activist Mahatma] Gandhi to give his beliefs an aura of respectability in the mainstream eye. If society is already in favor of violence across the board, and pacifism is revolutionary enough to fundamentally challenge our society and its ingrained oppressions, why does Czolgosz warrant hatred while Gandhi warrants approval?

Pacifists also harbor delusions about the decency of the state and, subconsciously, about the amount of protection their privileges will afford them. Students leading the occupation of Tiananmen Square in "Autonomous Beijing" [during protests against the Chinese government in 1989] thought that their "revolutionary" government would not open fire on them if they remained a peaceful, loyal opposition. "The students' nearly complete misunderstanding of the nature of legitimacy under bureaucratic power and the illusion that the Party could be negotiated with, left them defenseless both in terms of the theoretical means of describing their undertaking and in regards to the narrow practice of civil disobedience it led them to adopt," [according to writer Burt Green]. Thus, when the students who had put themselves in control of the movement refused to arm themselves (unlike many in the working-class suburbs, who were less educated and more intelligent), the whole movement was vulnerable, and Autonomous Beijing was crushed by the tanks of the People's Liberation Army. The students at Kent State [where several protestors were killed by members of the National Guard in 1970] were similarly shocked, even as the same government that killed a paltry number of them was massacring millions of people in Indochina [during the Vietnam War] without consequence or hesitation.

All Violence Is Not the Same

In the end, nonviolence has all the intellectual depth of a media sound bite. Pacifism requires a very vague, broad, loaded, and non-analytical term—*violence*—to take on a scientific precision. After all, not racism, not sexism, not homophobia, not authoritarianism, but violence, must be the critical axis of our actions. *Why would we take pledges of anti-racism before a march, or make participation in a movement contingent on being respectful of women, queer people, and trans people, when we can take far less divisive pledges of nonviolence?* The likelihood that most supporters of nonviolence codes have never even asked this question goes a long way toward demonstrating the limitation of pacifist thinking. So pacifists ignore real divisions such as white privilege and instead make baseless and potentially racist/classist distinctions between cutting a lock during a pre-announced demonstration so that protestors can conduct a die-in [a form of protest where protestors simulate being dead] on a military base and smashing a window under cover of a riot so that a ghetto dweller can get food and money to take care of her family. Significantly, pacifists do not make the critical distinction between the structural, institutional, and systemically permitted personal violence of the state (the state being understood in a broad sense to include the functions of the economy and patriarchy) and the individualized social violence of the "criminal" sort or collective social violence of the "revolutionary" sort, aimed at destroying the far greater violence of the state. Pretending that all violence is the same is very convenient for supposedly antiviolence privileged people who benefit from the violence of the state and have much to lose from the violence of revolution.

Periodical and Internet Sources Bibliography

The following articles have been selected to supplement the diverse views presented in this chapter.

Sherry F. Colb	"Abortion Clinic Violence: Is 'Pro-Life' Murder an Oxymoron?" FindLaw, January 9, 2008. http://writ.news.findlaw.com.
Consistent Life	"Reflections on Abortion and Pacifist Principles." www.consistent-life.org.
Phil Dickens	"Why Pacifism Is Morally Indefensible," *Property Is Theft!* (blog), March 14, 2010. http://propertyistheft.wordpress.com.
G. William Domhoff	"Social Movements and Strategic Nonviolence," Who Rules America? March 2005. http://sociology.ucsc.edu/whorulesamerica.
Michael J. Faris	"Pacifist and Pro-Choice," *A Collage of Citations* (blog), January 22, 2007. http://michaeljfaris.com.
George Lakey	"Nonviolent Action as the Sword That Heals," Training for Change, March 2001. www.trainingforchange.org.
Ramesh Ponnuru	"Torture and Pacifism," *The Corner* (blog), January 4, 2010. http://corner.nationalreview.com.
Julian Sanchez	"The Spectre of Pacifism," *Julian Sanchez* (blog), January 4, 2010. www.juliansanchez.com.
Claire Schaeffer-Duffy	"Stammering About Abortion," *National Catholic Reporter*, January 16, 2010.
Marc Thiessen	"Re: Americans Support Waterboarding," *The Corner* (blog), January 2, 2010. http://corner.nationalreview.com.

For Further Discussion

Chapter 1

1. Mark D. Tooley accuses pacifists of being too idealistic and of failing to address "the real world." How does the Mennonite Church Canada respond to the charge of being too idealistic? Is the church's response convincing, or does it seem impracticable?
2. Which of the writers in this chapter do you think would have supported U.S. entry into World War II? Into Vietnam? Can you think of a war that you are certain Mark D. Tooley would not support (would he support a nuclear first strike, for example)? Can you think of one that the Mennonite Church Canada, William Witt, or Paul Rasor would support? Explain the reasoning behind your conclusions.

Chapter 2

1. How do you think Brant Rosen would try to solve the conflict between Israel and Islamic nations in the Middle East? How would David B. Kopel try to solve it? What about WorldNetDaily? Which of these approaches do you think would be most successful, and why?
2. Jeanette Shin argues that the Buddha did not shun people who served in the military. Does it follow from this that the Buddha condoned violence? Explain your answer.

Chapter 3

1. In his viewpoint, Robert M. Price says that he stopped being a pacifist when he heard a minister renounce the right to defend his wife from rape. Does Bryan Caplan believe that pacifists must renounce the right to personal

self-defense? Do any of Price's arguments seem effective against Caplan's commonsense version of pacifism?

2. In the anecdote about the minister defending his wife from rape, Robert M. Price suggests that the renunciation of all violence may be dangerous to women. Would Ladd Everitt agree that pacifism endangers those who are disadvantaged and those who face discrimination? Would Rachel Shabi agree that pacifism and women's safety are incompatible? Based on these discussions, do you think that pacifism overall is a philosophy that helps or harms women? Explain your answer.

Chapter 4

1. Guli Fager argues that people like James R. Kelly who link peace and the pro-life movement are dupes of people who use the pro-life movement to try to oppress women. Are Kelly's arguments logically invalidated because some people who agree with him have different motives? Does Kelly worry that his pro-life arguments will be undermined because of some involved in the pro-life movement? Explain your answers.
2. Do you think you can logically approve of torture while opposing all war? Can you acknowledge the need for war while rejecting the use of torture? Could you approve of defending yourself with violence while rejecting all torture? Explain your answer in light of the viewpoints by V. Henry T. Nguyen, Joe Carter, and Sam Harris.

Organizations to Contact

The editors have compiled the following list of organizations concerned with the issues debated in this book. The descriptions are derived from materials provided by the organizations. All have publications or information available for interested readers. The list was compiled on the date of publication of the present volume; the information provided here may change. Be aware that many organizations take several weeks or longer to respond to inquiries, so allow as much time as possible.

Amnesty International USA (AIUSA)
5 Penn Plaza, New York, NY 10001
(212) 807-8400 • fax: (212) 627-1451
e-mail: aimember@aiusa.org
website: www.aiusa.org

Amnesty International is a grassroots activist organization with more than 1.8 million members worldwide. Amnesty International USA (AIUSA) is the United States branch of the global organization. Amnesty International undertakes research and action to prevent and end grave abuses of human rights including the rights to physical and mental integrity, freedom of conscience and expression, and freedom from discrimination. The group's website contains a section on human rights, with a twelve-point program to prevent torture, and a search of AIUSA's website produces issue briefs and other materials on war crimes, war, peace, and torture.

Buddhist Peace Fellowship
PO Box 3470, Berkeley, CA 94703
(510) 655-6169 • fax: (510) 655-1369
e-mail: membership@bpf.org
website: www.bpf.org

Buddhist Peace Fellowship (BPF) is a community of Buddhist practitioners established to promote social justice and change. It offers a public witness for peace through its practice; raises humanitarian concerns among Buddhist communities; and brings a Buddhist perspective to contemporary peace and environmental and social justice movements. It publishes the twice yearly *Turning Wheel* magazine, and its website includes articles, updates, and resources about peace and social justice issues.

Carnegie Endowment for International Peace (CEIP)
1779 Massachusetts Avenue NW
Washington, DC 20036-2103
(202) 483-7600 • fax: (202) 483-1840
e-mail: info@carnegieendowment.org
website: www.ceip.org

The Carnegie Endowment for International Peace (CEIP) is a private, nonprofit organization that is dedicated to advancing cooperation between nations and promoting active international engagement by the United States. CEIP publishes the quarterly journal *Foreign Policy*, a magazine of international politics and economics that is published in several languages and reaches readers in more than 120 countries. Its website includes numerous news articles and publications, such as *Iran: A View from Moscow* and *The Challenge of USAID.*

Cato Institute
1000 Massachusetts Avenue NW
Washington, DC 20001-5403
(202) 842-0200 • fax: (202) 842-3490
website: www.cato.org

The CATO Institute is a libertarian public policy research foundation dedicated to peace and limited government intervention in foreign affairs. It publishes numerous reports and periodicals, including *Policy Analysis* and *Cato Policy Review*, both of which discuss US policy in regional conflicts. Its website contains a searchable database of institute articles, news, and commentary, including "US Out of South Korea" and "Peace? The Promise of Peace? Eh, Close Enough."

Council on Foreign Relations
58 East Sixty-eighth Street, New York, NY 10065
(212) 434-9400 • fax: (212) 434-9800
website: www.cfr.org

The Council on Foreign Relations specializes in foreign affairs and studies the international aspects of American political and economic policies and problems. Its journal *Foreign Affairs*, published five times a year, includes analyses of current conflicts around the world. Its website publishes editorials, interviews, and articles, including "The Price of World Peace" and "Time for U.S. Middle East Peace Plan?"

Human Rights Watch (HRW)
1630 Connecticut Avenue NW, Suite 500
Washington, DC 20009
(202) 612-4321 • fax: (202) 612-4333
e-mail: hrwdc@hrw.org
website: www.hrw.org

Human Rights Watch (HRW) is an independent, nongovernmental organization supported by contributions from private individuals and foundations worldwide. HRW conducts fact-finding investigations into human rights abuses and publishes those findings in dozens of books and reports. HRW also meets with government officials to urge changes in policy and practice and provides up-to-the-minute information about conflicts while they are under way. The organization's website contains numerous publications including news articles, legislative statements, and reports, such as "Getting Away with Torture? Command Responsibility for the U.S. Abuse of Detainees" and "Harsh War, Harsh Peace: Abuses by al-Shabaab, the Transitional Federal Government, and AMISOM in Somalia."

Kroc Institute for International Peace Studies
100 Hesburg Center for International Studies
University of Notre Dame, Notre Dame, IN 46556-5677
(547) 631-6970 • fax: (547) 631-6973

e-mail: krocinst@nd.edu
website: www.nd.edu/~krocinst

The Kroc Institute for International Peace Studies follows the Catholic social tradition of promoting the prevention of violence and war. It publishes the journal *Report* twice each year. A database of its research papers is available on its website.

Mennonite Church Canada
600 Shaftesbury Boulevard, Winnipeg, Manitoba R3P 0M4 Canada
(204) 888-6781 • fax: (204) 831-5675
e-mail: office@mennonitechurch.ca
website: www.mennonitechurch.ca

The Mennonite Church is a Christian denomination with a historic commitment to peace and nonviolence. Mennonite Church Canada is an umbrella organization for Mennonite churches in the country. It publishes the biweekly Anabaptist/Mennonite publication *Canadian Mennonite*, which can be found on its website. Mennonite Church Canada's website also includes information about programs, news, and resources relating to the Mennonite Church and its work in social justice and peace.

Resource Center for Nonviolence
515 Broadway, Santa Cruz, CA 95060
(831) 423-1626
e-mail: information@rcnv.org
website: www.rcnv.org

The Resource Center for Nonviolence was founded in 1976 and promotes nonviolence as a force for personal and social change. The center provides speakers, workshops, leadership development, and nonviolence training programs. Its website publishes editorials, essays, news articles, and reports.

United for Peace and Justice (UFPJ)
PO Box 607, Times Square Station, New York, NY 10108

(212) 868-5545 • fax: (646) 723-0996
website: www.unitedforpeace.org

United for Peace and Justice (UFPJ) opposes preemptive wars of aggression and rejects any drive to expand US control over other nations and strip Americans of rights at home under the cover of fighting terrorism and spreading democracy. It rejects the use of war and racism to concentrate power in the hands of the few. The UFPJ website publishes recent anti-war events, news articles, and essays.

Bibliography of Books

Peter Ackerman and Jack DuVall	*A Force More Powerful: A Century of Non-Violent Conflict*. New York: Palgrave, 2000.
Sanam Naraghi Anderlini	*Women Building Peace: What They Do, Why It Matters*. Boulder, CO: Lynne Rienner Publishers, 2007.
Bob Brecher	*Torture and the Ticking Bomb*. Malden, MA: Blackwell Publishing, 2007.
Heloise Brown	*The Truest Form of Patriotism: Pacifist Feminism in Britain, 1870–1902*. Manchester, UK: Manchester University Press, 2004.
Perry Bush	*Two Kingdoms, Two Loyalties: Mennonite Pacifism in Modern America*. Baltimore, MD: John Hopkins University Press, 1998.
J. Daryl Charles	*Between Pacifism and Jihad: Just War and Christian Tradition*. Downers Grove, IL: InterVarsity Press, 2005.
Ward Churchill	*Pacifism as Pathology: Reflections on the Role of Armed Struggle in North America*. Oakland, CA: AK Press, 2007.
Cynthia Cockburn	*From Where We Stand: War, Women's Activism, and Feminist Analysis*. New York: Zed Books, 2007.

John Dear	*A Persistent Peace: One Man's Struggle for a Nonviolent World.* Chicago, IL: Loyola Press, 2008.
John Dear	*Put Down Your Sword: Answering the Gospel Call to Creative Nonviolence.* Grand Rapids, MI: William B. Eerdmans Publishing Co., 2008.
Jean Bethke Elshtain	*Just War Against Terror: The Burden of American Power in a Violent World.* New York: Basic Books, 2003.
Paul R. Fleischman	*The Buddha Taught Nonviolence, Not Pacifism.* Seattle, WA: Pariyatti Press, 2002.
Nicholas Fotion	*War and Ethics: A New Just War Theory.* New York: Continuum Books, 2007.
Charles Guthrie and Michael Quinlan	*Just War: The Just War Tradition: Ethics in Modern Warfare.* New York: Walker Publishing Company, 2007.
Sam Harris	*The End of Faith: Religion, Terror, and the Future of Reason.* New York: W.W. Norton & Company, 2005.
Kristin E. Heyer	*Prophetic & Public: The Social Witness of U.S. Catholicism.* Washington, DC: Georgetown University Press, 2006.
Dustin Ells Howes	*Toward a Credible Pacifism: Violence and the Possibilities of Politics.* Albany: State University of New York Press, 2009.

Mark Kurlansky	*Nonviolence: The History of a Dangerous Idea*. New York: Modern Library, 2008.
Peter Marshall	*Demanding the Impossible: A History of Anarchism*. Oakland, CA: PM Press, 2010.
Marian Mollin	*Radical Pacifism in Modern America: Egalitarianism and Protest*. Philadelphia, PA: University of Pennsylvania Press, 2006.
John D. Roth	*Choosing Against War: A Christian View: A Love Stronger than Our Fears*. Intercourse, PA: Good Books, 2002.
David R. Smock	*Perspectives on Pacifism: Christian, Jewish, and Muslim Views on Nonviolence and International Conflict*. Washington, DC: United States Institute of Peace Press, 1995.
Evelyn Wilcock	*Pacifism and the Jews*. Gloucestershire, UK: Hawthorn Press, 1994.
Howard Zinn	*The Power of Nonviolence: Writings by Advocates of Peace*. Boston, MA: Beacon Press, 2002.
Stephen Zunes, Sarah Beth Asher, and Lester R. Kurtz, eds.	*Nonviolent Social Movements: A Geographical Perspective*. Malden, MA: Blackwell Publishers, 1999.

Index

B

C

N

Q

R